Cambridge Elements

Elements in Austrian Economics
edited by
Peter Boettke
George Mason University

INSTITUTIONAL DIVERSITY AND THE ECONOMIC CALCULATION DEBATE

The Feasibility Issue Revisited

Paul Dragos Aligica
*George Mason University and
University of Bucharest*

Adrian Miroiu
The Romanian Academy

Shaftesbury Road, Cambridge CB2 8EA, United Kingdom

One Liberty Plaza, 20th Floor, New York, NY 10006, USA

477 Williamstown Road, Port Melbourne, VIC 3207, Australia

314–321, 3rd Floor, Plot 3, Splendor Forum, Jasola District Centre, New Delhi – 110025, India

103 Penang Road, #05–06/07, Visioncrest Commercial, Singapore 238467

Cambridge University Press is part of Cambridge University Press & Assessment, a department of the University of Cambridge.

We share the University's mission to contribute to society through the pursuit of education, learning and research at the highest international levels of excellence.

www.cambridge.org
Information on this title: www.cambridge.org/9781009677479

DOI: 10.1017/9781009677431

© Paul Dragos Aligica and Adrian Miroiu 2025

This publication is in copyright. Subject to statutory exception and to the provisions of relevant collective licensing agreements, no reproduction of any part may take place without the written permission of Cambridge University Press & Assessment.

When citing this work, please include a reference to the DOI 10.1017/9781009677431

First published 2025

A catalogue record for this publication is available from the British Library

ISBN 978-1-009-67747-9 Hardback
ISBN 978-1-009-67748-6 Paperback
ISSN 2399-651X (online)
ISSN 2514-3867 (print)

Cambridge University Press & Assessment has no responsibility for the persistence or accuracy of URLs for external or third-party internet websites referred to in this publication and does not guarantee that any content on such websites is, or will remain, accurate or appropriate.

For EU product safety concerns, contact us at Calle de José Abascal, 56, 1°, 28003 Madrid, Spain, or email eugpsr@cambridge.org

Institutional Diversity and the Economic Calculation Debate

The Feasibility Issue Revisited

Elements in Austrian Economics

DOI: 10.1017/9781009677431
First published online: July 2025

Paul Dragos Aligica
*George Mason University and
University of Bucharest*

Adrian Miroiu
The Romanian Academy

Author for correspondence: Paul Dragos Aligica, pdragos@mercatus.gmu.edu

Abstract: This Element brings together the problems of economic calculation, institutional diversity, and institutional feasibility, arguing that these themes are deeply interconnected and mutually reinforcing. Building on recent developments in institutional theory, political economy, social philosophy, and logical analysis, the Element revisits the classic debates surrounding alternative economic and governance systems. The discussion is organized around three core elements: (1) an overview of recent developments in institutional theory and social philosophy, that driven by technological advances have revitalized debates on alternative economic and governance systems; (2) a reexamination of the economic calculation debate, tracing its evolution from Austrian economics to a broader theoretical synthesis incorporating institutional political economy and conflict theory; and (3) a discussion of the formal, logical, and philosophical foundations for thinking about feasibility and realizability, offering analytical tools for evaluating the plausibility of institutional alternatives within specific historical and social contexts.

Keywords: institutions, governance, feasibility, comparative economic systems, market process, public choice, political philosophy, institutional epistemology, possibilism, non-ideal theory

© Paul Dragos Aligica and Adrian Miroiu 2025

ISBNs: 9781009677479 (HB), 9781009677486 (PB), 9781009677431 (OC)
ISSNs: 2399-651X (online), 2514-3867 (print)

Contents

1 Introduction — 1

2 Institutional Diversity, Institutional Feasibility, and the Challenge of Possibilism — 7

3 Institutional Structure and Performance: Comparative Economic Systems, Institutional Analysis, and the Endogenization of Feasibility — 17

4 The Economic Calculation Debate Revisited: Exchange, Rivalry, and Institutions — 28

5 The Feasible: Conceptualization and Formalization at the Boundaries of Ideal Theory — 47

6 Conclusions — 64

References — 67

1 Introduction

The economic calculation debate, the problem of institutional diversity, and the issue of feasibility are intertwined in profound ways. Any discussion of the problem of economic calculation inevitably leads to a discussion about alternative institutional arrangements, and the problem of alternative institutional arrangements sooner or later leads to the problem of feasibility. Similarly, any discussion of the feasibility of alternative institutional arrangements must address sooner or later the challenges associated with rational economic calculation and efficacy in decision-making. This "Cambridge Elements" volume brings together these three tracks, revisiting them in light of the relevant developments and their converging significance for contemporary theoretical and applied discussions. The structure of the volume brings therefore together the building blocks of this cluster of themes around three "elements":

(1) An overview and discussion of the evolutions in institutional theory and social philosophy that, fueled by the new circumstances created by the technological revolution (especially the breakthroughs in information technology), have reopened the debate regarding alternative economic and governance systems.
(2) A discussion of the economic calculation debate and an overview of how the theoretical apparatus associated with it has evolved, building around the traditional Austrian economics conceptualization, a social theory that combines institutionalist political economy and an original type of conflict theory.
(3) An overview and discussion of the formal – logical and philosophical – structures of thinking about feasibility and realizability as benchmarks for discourses on institutional alternatives and the possibility or impossibility of social processes taking place in specific historical and social circumstances.

The objective of the volume is not to provide a solution to the "feasibility issue" or to claim the final word on the "economic calculation problem." Instead, it aims to offer an up-to-date overview of what the coauthors consider some of the main themes relevant to an informed approach to the topic at his moment. The goal is to give readers insights from these different but converging tracks as well as a sense of how the tools and conceptual frameworks have evolved to provide a more nuanced and better-grounded approach to the contemporary discussions regarding institutional alternatives and their feasibility.

Each of the main sections can be read independently, but as the reader may note, there are cross-references and underlying themes that support each other across disciplinary and domain divides. In conjunction, they offer a unified perspective. Each section reflects on the current state of the relevant discussions in its subfield. At the same time, the selection of what is considered relevant, along with the specific angle, approach, and interpretation given, is obviously influenced by our priors and subjective perspectives. Therefore, we do not claim that the overview provided in this volume is comprehensive or that it is articulated from a privileged, unbiased stance. It should be read simply as an attempt to provide what we consider to be the main elements of an informed conversation about the problems of feasibility and alternative economic and governance systems in the current circumstances of the beginning of the twenty-first century.

The starting point is a familiar and intuitively clear set of questions: What are the core defining features of political-economic systems that make possible economic development and good governance? How vast is the range of possible arrangements that make possible certain forms of institutional performance? What is realizable and what is not when it comes to imagining alternative economic and political systems? For a long time, the debate generated by these questions was organized around two major concepts, each standing for two institutional packages or sets: one labeled "capitalism," the other "socialism." It was recognized that there was some diversity within each, but the debate – as illustrated most clearly by the field of comparative economic systems – was mainly between the cores of the two sets, not between the variations around the cores or other imaginable alternatives. With the collapse of the socialist block in 1989 and the triumph of capitalism, it was concluded that an answer was given by the very developments in real life: Socialism – as the economic calculation argument regarding the possibility of Socialism had predicted – was indeed not feasible.

Yet, since then, two things have happened: First, it was a shift of attention to the diversity within capitalist, liberal-democratic systems, and then even more, as the technological revolution seems to have created the conditions for the institutional feasibility frontier to shift upward, an explosion of interest in alternative economic and governance systems. The institutional feasibility frontier refers to the set of institutional arrangements that are viable or implementable given the technological, economic, and social constraints of a given time. It defines the boundary between feasible and infeasible institutions, meaning that as technology advances, this boundary can shift, making new institutional models possible that were previously impractical.

Second, a parallel development within the institutional theory research program brought to the fore the problems of institutional diversity and the contextual nature of institutional performance: "context matters." The outcome was a somewhat "revisionist" thesis, articulated more and more insistently: The institutional diversity of economic performance is rather vast, or in any case, vaster than the adepts of free market capitalism claim. This is a thesis of major potential impact because it reopens the direction of inquiry and debate that was dormant or even considered closed by 1989 and the collapse of real-life socialism in Eastern Europe.

In the maximalist interpretation, one could easily take a step further and argue for the plausibility of configurations of presumably viable institutions and economic systems that may go beyond the core features that we associate with capitalism and liberal democratic governance. Once the issues of "institutional diversity" and "context relevance" are in the picture, a reopening of the old Capitalism vs. Socialism debate is only one small step away, as the AI technosocialism thesis has demonstrated (Boettke and Candela 2023). And from there, the next step comes naturally: a debate about the wide range of institutional alternatives and the feasibility of alternative governance and economic systems way outside the limited range of the institutional imagination of the twentieth century.

Thus, in the light of the "institutional diversity" perspective reinforced by the "contextual" interpretation of institutional processes, a stronger challenging thesis has emerged: It is plausible to imagine a larger range of institutional configurations, of feasible economic systems, than the classical comparative economic systems literature indicated. There is no unique core-set of configurations of institutions associated structurally and functionally with economic performance.

In a sense, these developments brought to the fore something that Albert O. Hirschman (1971) captured aptly under the notion of "possibilism." Seen as an ethos and approach, possibilism emphasizes the potential for change and innovation within socio-economic systems, even under constraints or in less than ideal conditions. It comes with a rejection of deterministic or pessimistic views and advances the belief that agents in economic and social contexts have the ability to creatively respond to challenges. Therefore, possibilism is not just a philosophical stance but an ideological worldview that transcends mere economic and social analysis. It advocates for a broader exploration of potential solutions and pathways for progress, resonating profoundly with the climate of opinion of the current age.

Possibilism fits thus very well with a certain contemporary worldview: A stance that emphasizes the role of human agency and creativity in overcoming constraints, suggesting that individuals and societies are not merely adaptive recipients of circumstances but active creators of solutions. It asserts that outcomes are not preordained by structures or systems but are open to change through human action. Possibilism recognizes the significance of context in shaping possibilities, positing that opportunities and solutions are context-dependent, and what is not possible in one situation may be in another. Indeed, this concept inherently carries an optimistic outlook on the potential for positive change, even in seemingly difficult situations. It encourages exploring a range of possibilities, often leading to innovative and effective solutions, if sufficient intensity is applied to the efforts. It is thus deeply satisfying and motivating.

Yet, given the harsh reality that structural constraints in society, economics, or human nature can significantly limit agency and creativity, how does Hirschman's concept realistically address these limitations? Can the inherent optimism in possibilism lead to underestimating challenges or ignoring potential negative outcomes, thereby compromising realism in planning and decision-making? Are human institutions and the governance and economic systems that malleable?

Setting aside the temptations of an ideological debate, these intellectual developments raise a very important analytical question: What are the limits of institutional diversity when it comes to economic (or governance) performance? Are there any limits? If one accepts the configurational, combinatorial, and contextual analysis of the institutional diversity perspective, how far could one go in presuming various forms of institutional performance for the emerging systems and combinations? Is there any way to conceptually or theoretically draw a line between combinations of features, rules, and institutions leading to economic performance, and those that do not? Between what will work and what it will not work? How do we discern ex ante between what should be feasible and what not? It seems intuitively clear that such limits exist, but how could one derive them?

In brief, how could one define what is possible and what is impossible, what is feasible and what is not, in a world of institutional diversity and contextual performance? How should we think in a consistent way about institutional feasibility? This study is an attempt to revisit and re-articulate an informed approach to this challenge. While not claiming to offer the solution, it aims to contribute to reigniting a conceptually and philosophically anchored discussion regarding these crucial questions. We are entering a new stage in the evolution of our thinking in this respect and our volume charts some of the most significant elements of this transition.

Indeed, over the past three decades, the concept of feasibility has become increasingly significant in political economy, institutional theory, and the social sciences. This heightened focus is not just theoretical; it presents a practical challenge. As we have noted, the evolving ideological and intellectual landscape has brought to the forefront again the question of what is feasible in economic and political systems, making it a pressing issue for researchers and practitioners alike.

As noted, technological advancements have significantly expanded the realm of institutional possibilities. The latest technological innovations are enabling institutional solutions and arrangements that until recently were not cost-effective or even conceivable. This shift has opened new pathways for how institutions can operate and interact, potentially leading to more efficient, and innovative organizational structures and governance models. In brief, the transformative power of technology is redefining what is feasible within institutional frameworks, challenging old paradigms, and encouraging the exploration of novel approaches in various sectors.

Concurrently and not totally unrelated to that, the cultural environment and the climate of opinion are currently undergoing significant changes, marked by a growing desire for social transformation. This shift is characterized by an impatience with the existing state of affairs and a strong inclination toward experimentation. Society is increasingly open to exploring new ideas and approaches, demonstrating a readiness to challenge and reevaluate the status quo. At the same time, the institutional and social memory of recent generations concerning past experiments and their associated trade-offs is becoming increasingly faint. The communist and the national socialist experiments and experiences look more and more like "ancient history." This fading memory may impact the way new generations approach and understand the complexities, trade-offs, and consequences of institutional changes, radical social transformation processes, or even social reforms. There's a growing lack of comprehension about the precautionary principle's application and significance, particularly in the context of social and economic risks. Yet, a realistic, empirically and historically informed understanding of this principle is crucial for recognizing potential social and economic consequences before they materialize.

Each of these issues is both matters of concern and exciting intellectual challenges. They motivate a renewed effort to revisit and better articulate our fundamental approaches to the problem of institutional analysis and design, especially along the lines of the desirability and feasibility of alternative institutional arrangements. Our volume should thus be seen as a contribution to this effort.

The volume starts (Section 2) with a discussion of the developments that have been taking place in the realm of ideas and academic debate, at the interface between politics, economics, and philosophy. These developments have brought to salience the problem of feasibility, or more specifically, the problem of institutional feasibility. In a sense, the section will elaborate and give bibliographical anchoring to the observations made in this introductory section which set up the stage for the volume.

After charting the thematic and conceptual territory, the volume advances three different tracks of engagement:

The first track (Section 3) will examine the twin challenges of possibilism and feasibility within the context of recent developments in New Institutional Economics (NIE). Utilizing two key frameworks – the Koopmans–Montias Comparative Economic Systems (CES) framework and the Ostroms' Institutional Analysis and Development (IAD) Framework – we will explore how NIE has redefined our understanding of governance and social systems. The section will show how this understanding naturally arises from the institutionalist revolution, enhancing our ability to conceptualize problems of institutional feasibility, while also revealing the complexities of predicting governance viability. Additionally, we will discuss the innovative ideas of endogenizing feasibility, which redefines the search for feasibility as a dynamic process of institutional epistemology geared to adaptation and evolution.

The second track (Section 4) is centered around the economic calculation debate, a pivotal moment in the history of social sciences and governance studies, a debate regarding the feasibility of Communism, arguably the largest "natural" social experiment ever undertaken in human history. The section treats this intellectual and scholarly dispute as an epitome and as a crucial case study for all subsequent discussions about institutional design and institutional feasibility. At stake is a formidable problem: Understanding how to conceptualize and approach proposals for radical institutional changes. Even more challenging: How to assess potential institutional performance in the absence of any relevant precedent, case study, or empirical evidence. That is to say, how to develop a methodical approach to conjectures about institutional feasibility, in conditions of structural uncertainty and dynamic complexity.

The third track (Section 5) takes a different direction, concentrating on the conceptualization and the formal apparatus to be applied in our efforts to capture and understand the logic of our statements regarding what is feasible and what is not. Without denying that the formalism of general equilibrium has a role in dealing with the issue, it shifts the focus at the broader and deeper level. It deals with the ways of thinking about and defining feasibility, exploring various angles of approach to this complex issue, and mobilizing the perspectives and the tools of symbolic logic and analytical philosophy.

The volume wraps-up by presenting – based on the insights gained in the previous sections – a set of general conclusions regarding the problem of institutional feasibility, seen both as a notion and as a phenomenon crucial for addressing the new challenges – political, economic, and institutional – of the twenty-first century.

2 Institutional Diversity, Institutional Feasibility, and the Challenge of Possibilism

For a significant period, the exploration of the desirability and feasibility of alternative institutional and economic systems was primarily focused on capitalism and socialism. After the fall of socialist regimes in 1989, socialism was widely regarded as unfeasible, effectively ending the debate on its viability. Capitalism appeared to be the only remaining viable system. Shortly after, the emergence of NIE redefined the approach to comparative economic systems and institutional analysis. This shift, combined with the impact of technological and intellectual developments following the 2008 financial crisis, reignited discussions on the viability and desirability of systems alternative to market capitalism and liberal democracy. These trends set the stage for our current discussion.

At the heart of the renewed interest in alternative systems discourse are the twin themes of institutional diversity and contextual possibilism. These concepts have gained prominence in recent literature, casting the problem of feasibility in a new light. They offered a fresh restart to the conjectures regarding how different economic and political systems can be viable under varying contexts and conditions, challenging the previously held notions about the unfeasibility of alternatives to capitalism. The problem of feasibility was thus reopened. A closer look at the theories and literature driving this development will put us in the position to better understand the nature of the revamped challenges posed by the feasibility problem in the new circumstances, as well as the conceptual and analytical background of these developments.

Over the course of the last thirty years, there were many attempts to address capitalism emerging as a victor from the Cold War and bring more substance to the task of *comparative* analysis of capitalistic systems. The "Varieties of Capitalism" literature, notably starting with Hall & Soskice's 2001 work, was one of the most successful such attempts. It introduced a fundamental distinction between liberal and coordinated market economies based on the analysis of five coordination spheres (Amable and Petit 2001; Amable 2003; Pryor 2005; Crouch et al. 2005; Coates 2005; Allen 2006; Cernat 2006; Lane and Myant 2007) and underscored the idea that there is no singular recipe for economic performance (Hall and Soskice 2001, 21). Both liberal and coordinated market economies are capable of achieving satisfactory economic performance, although they may vary in other performance dimensions. In the "Varieties of Capitalism" literature, the idea of institutional diversity is thus central to understanding the different ways in which market economies are organized across various capitalist countries, recognizing that there is no "one-size-fits-all" model of capitalism.

From a somewhat different perspective, synthesizing the insights gained via a line of research mostly focused on developing economies, Rodrik (2007) has also made a similar claim. One of his books, suggestively titled *One Economics, Many Recipes*, makes the argument that "appropriate growth policies are almost always context-specific" (2007, 4), and thus argues against "the tendency of many economists to offer advice based on simple rules of thumb, regardless of context (privatize this, liberalize that)," which, in his view, "is a derogation rather than a proper application of neoclassical economic principles" (2007, 3).

In Rodrik's framing of the matter, context dependence follows precisely from paying attention to individuals and processes of emergence: "Social phenomena can best be understood by considering them to be an aggregation of purposeful behavior by individuals – in their roles as consumer, producer, investor, politician, and so on – interacting with each other and acting under the constraints that their environment imposes" (2007, 3). Consequently, context dependence occurs "not because economics works differently in different settings, but because the *environments* in which households, firms, and investors operate differ in terms of the opportunities and constraints they present" (2007, 4).

The focus on context reinforces and is reinforced by a theoretical approach in which the metaphor of the "rules of the game" is the dominant keyword. Over the last decades, the metaphor of the "rules of the game," inspired by game theory, has had a profound influence on social sciences, particularly in the realms of economics, political science, and sociology (North 1990; Ostrom et al. 1994). This metaphor, which conceptualizes social interactions as games with certain rules that players (individuals, firms, or governments) must follow, offers a framework for understanding strategic decision-making and behavioral patterns in various contexts. In economics, it has been instrumental in analyzing market dynamics, competitive strategies, and bargaining scenarios. Political science has utilized it to examine the strategic interactions between different political actors, including voters, interest groups, and political parties. Overall, the integration of game theory's "rules of the game" metaphor into social sciences has significantly enhanced the analytical tools available to researchers, allowing for more precise and nuanced explorations of human behavior and societal structures.

Any approach to distinguishing between the "rules of the game" and "the game" itself leads to a two-level analysis: the meta-level, where the rules, structures, and environmental constraints are defined, and the micro-level, where individual actions and interactions occur within these constraints. Such an approach encourages the idea that while economic principles and basic human motivation remain relatively constant, their application and effects vary based on the specific context – the opportunities and limitations present in each environment. Therefore, a comprehensive understanding of economic phenomena requires an analysis that accounts for both the overarching rules and the individual, context-dependent actions.

To sum up, the origins of this novel attention given to the role of contextual and circumstantial configurations of variables in social research are diverse and come from different disciplines and research areas. We have witnessed emerging an entire domain devoted to it. Interest grew to the point that a thematic *Oxford Handbook* was dedicated to it (Goodin and Tilly 2008). As Goodin and Tilly (2008, 20) noted, an increasingly larger number of scholars concur that one needs to "shift attention away from empirically grounded general laws to repeated processes and toward efficacious causal mechanisms that operate at multiple scales but produce their aggregate effects through their concatenation, sequences, and interaction with initial conditions." This perspective recognizes that responses to many social science questions are typically contingent, often summarized by the phrase "it depends." Such an acknowledgment calls for a major rethinking of epistemic objectives, moving beyond the pursuit of general laws or generalized methodological skepticism. Goodin and Tilly advocate for "correcting for context," which involves situating an event, structure, or process within a broader interdependent set of elements (pp. 12–13). This approach emphasizes understanding how these elements interact and influence each other, thereby acknowledging the critical role of context in shaping social phenomena.

Arguably the strongest arguments regarding contextual analysis come, however, from the quarters of the NIE. The 1990s were a period of extraordinary development and synthesis of NIE, as recognized by the Nobel prizes received by Ronald Coase, Douglass North, Elinor Ostrom, and Oliver Williamson. The methods and rigor of institutional analysis have been taken to a new level (Williamson 1985; North 1990, 2005; Ostrom 1990, 2005, 2008; Miller 1992).

The conceptual rigor offered by NIE was derived from its incorporation of the analytics of microeconomics and rational choice in a theoretical framework combining macro- and micro- level approaches (Coleman 1990). Bringing individual-level processes into the analysis filters out a lot of the arbitrariness of a purely aggregative perspective, and illuminates mechanisms for social and political change that could bolster and give even more traction to the institutional diversity and contextualist challenge. Thus, in the new NIE approach, one may identify with clarity the methodological and theoretical contours of the entire change of epistemological and methodological perspective, bringing the problem of "context" to the forefront in social research. Let us take a step further and take a closer look at NIE and how the unfolding of this complex research program to its ultimate implications has reopened the problem of institutional feasibility in the postcommunist era.

2.1 The Institutional Revolution and a Relatively Unexpected Turn

Among the new institutionalist economics luminaries, E. Ostrom's position is emblematic for the NIE insights in multiple ways. Her work documents how these insights emerged naturally from traditional research programs based on public choice and rational choice theory. Ostrom, one of the first authors to take seriously the challenge of thinking in methodical ways of dealing with contextual and on-the-ground factors and the problems fieldwork and observational research pose, was in fact summing up an entire cycle of research on collective action and commons when she noted that "contextual variables are essential for understanding the initial growth and sustainability of collective action. That is to say, there were no one-size-fits-all institutions and no blueprint thinking when it comes to institutions" (Ostrom 1990, 33).

That was not quite the answer expected by many decades earlier when this research program was initiated, with strong epistemological and normative assumptions backing it. Let us take a closer look at the relevant developments leading to this conclusion, using Elinor Ostrom's work as a vehicle.

The origins and the best illustration of this point are in Ostrom's influential *Governing the Commons* (1990). The tragedy of the commons was usually explained by means of a straightforward mathematical model. If self-interested agents play a Prisoner's Dilemma (PD), it is rational for all to overuse the resource. But, as Ostrom points out, this model is deceptive in its simplicity, distracting one's attention from the place where the real action takes place: the PD model directs one's attention to agents playing *within* a *given* game, while, in fact, the real action is concerned with agents *setting up or changing* the game itself.

As Ostrom (1990, 6–7) put it, "What makes these models so dangerous – when they are used metaphorically as the foundation for policy – is that the constraints are assumed to be fixed in empirical settings, unless external authorities change them." When people actually find themselves in PD situations, they usually recognize both the potential benefits of cooperation and the cause of the prevalent social dysfunction. As a result, they often invent and implement various anti-free-riding rules that punish defection and set up conditions for credible commitments – hence changing the game from a PD game to a Stag Hunt or even a cooperation game.

The idea is both intuitive and based on empirical observations: Actual people in empirical settings are confronted with real-life constraints, and, even more, constraints that vary and may vary widely. Hence, various strategies and behaviors vary a lot. Ostrom has found that in many cases, despite the problematic incentives individuals face, groups of individuals manage to overcome these cooperation dilemmas. An additional critical insight coming from Ostrom's research program was how surprisingly vast was the variety of institutional arrangements it imagined and implemented by individuals and communities. The corollary was evident: When it comes to comparative institutional analysis of alternative arrangements, Ostrom stressed the need to go beyond strict dichotomization, such as state versus market or private versus public. The world as experienced is more subtle and complicated. Simple concepts of "state" or "market" are usually neglecting institutional details. Context matters, and context and institutional diversity go hand in hand.

The significance of Ostrom's conclusions and insights could be fully appreciated if we take a step back and see her work as part of a larger and even more ambitious program started in the 1960s and focuses on the problem of collective action. Its objective: to understand the nature, processes, and conditions of success of coordination and cooperation against the adverse and perverse incentives faced by social actors. This was indeed one of the most important research programs of twentieth-century social science, one of the best methodologically and analytically articulated social science investigation lines, extending over multiple disciplines and many decades. Ostrom was at the core of it, being one of the most influential scholars in the world in this respect.

Following this research program unfolding, we can see that years of inquiry have led to the emergence of the powerful epistemic and theoretic idea at the center of our argument: The circumstantial configurations of variables determining action arenas and action situations are crucial for the success or failure of collective actions. Also, they determine the variety of institutional solutions and institutional arrangements, their performance, and their success. Context matters. Collective action research has demonstrated that contextual analysis should be taken seriously as a distinct methodological, epistemological, and theoretical possibility. Institutional analysis is, in large part, contextual analysis. Feasibility analysis provides the link between the conceptual and theoretical frameworks involved and the contextual realities on the ground.

The importance of Ostrom's contribution in this respect is that she followed the argument to its ultimate logical and empirical implications and articulated explicitly the conclusions. To understand collective action is to understand how institutional, cultural, and biophysical contexts affect collective action situations. "Contextual variables are essential for understanding the initial growth and sustainability of collective action as well as the challenges that long-surviving, self-organized regimes must try to overcome," explains Ostrom. "More work is needed to explain how a large array of contextual variables affects the processes of teaching and evoking social norms; of informing participants about the behavior of others and their adherence to social norms; and of rewarding those who use social norms, such as reciprocity, trust, and fairness" (Ostrom 2000, 154).

This shift toward the diversity of configurations shaping human interactions and their collective action dimension has serious consequences for our approaches, models, and theories. In affirming that context matters, we get a more nuanced understanding, but at the same time, we are forced to confront the limitations of our approaches. From experimental research we learn that contextual factors affect the rate of individual contribution to public goods; from field research, we are alerted to the fact that "an immense number of contextual variables" may hinder or facilitate endogenous collective action (Ostrom 2000, 148). In brief, each further specification applied in order to capture context elements leads to increasingly difficult generalizations. As Ostrom (1998, 15) put it, "changes in one structural variable can lead to a cascade of changes in the others." Just an apparently minor change in the configuration or magnitude of a variable "may suffice to reverse the predicted outcome."

We thus come to recognize "how difficult it is to make simple bivariate hypotheses about the effect of one variable on the level of cooperation" (Ostrom 1998, 15). This volatility and the unpredictability it entails, raise serious doubts about the possibility of identifying the general social laws of collective action. Out of such investigative effort, one may gain a better understanding of the phenomenon, but no universal law, code, or general model comes to be isolated and specified. The laws of collective action are elusive. One may identify and document a variety of mechanisms, processes, and linkages relating to possible configurations of variables, but one remains very far away from the ambitions of the broad initial generalizations of the "Tragedy of the Commons" or the "Logic of Collective Action" of the early literature of Hardin and Olson .

2.2 General Theory and Institutional Design

All these conclusions are very important, indeed. Their implications for the way we think about social research and institutional theory and design are considerable. Consequently, in the years that have passed since the collective action research program of Ostrom was launched, social scientists have been increasingly put in the position to reconsider their efforts to build "the theory of collective action" based on "the laws of collective action." But they found out that "it is not possible to relate all structural variables in one large causal model, given the number of important variables" (Ostrom 1998, 14). Today, scholars are more than ever ready to acknowledge that "there are many different issues and many different kinds of collective action, and that one can shade into the other depending on the structural characteristics of the situation" (Marwell and Oliver 1993, 25). In fact, authors such as Oliver and Marwell (2001, 292–293) go as far as to suggest that there is no single and unitary social phenomenon under that label. One needs "a disciplined search for the distinctions among different types of collective action and the factors that distinguish them" (Poteete and Ostrom 2004).

These insights and lessons from the decades-long research program on collective action are undoubtedly relevant for social sciences in general, confirming similar observations and conclusions reached in other domains and parallel research lines. Goodin and Tilly (2008) effectively summarize their most profound epistemological significance. The effort to identify simple, general laws in social phenomena has produced limited results. While this approach is more successful at identifying empirical regularities, it falls short in providing or verifying comprehensive explanations. General patterns do exist in social life, but they do not occur on the scale or in the forms assumed by the "covering laws" models in social science. The epistemology and methods focused on uncovering these general social laws are poorly aligned with the complexities of empirical reality. As Clarke and Primo (2012) bluntly put it, today, nobody among those informed holds such an outdated and faulty understanding of how science operates. Instead, models, both theoretical and empirical, come to be pivotal for social inquiry. Therefore, an increasingly larger number of scholars agree that we need to "shift attention away from empirically grounded general laws to repeated processes and toward efficacious causal mechanisms that operate at multiple scales but produce their aggregate effects through their concatenation, sequences, and interaction with initial conditions" (Goodin and Tilly 2008, 20).

On similar lines, Russell Hardin (2002) presents a critique of the limitations inherent in the pursuit of general laws in the social sciences, a theme that resonates strongly with the ideas expressed by Goodin and Tilly (2008). Hardin argues that social phenomena are often too complex and variable to be distilled into universal laws, as the traditional scientific method might seek. This perspective aligns with the shift called for by Goodin and Tilly, away from empirically grounded general laws toward an emphasis on efficacious causal mechanisms. These mechanisms, operating across various scales, produce outcomes through their interactions with initial conditions and sequences. This approach acknowledges the indeterminate nature of social phenomena, as Hardin suggests, recognizing that outcomes in social science are often contingent on a complex array of factors that can vary widely across different contexts.

Hardin's exploration of indeterminacy in social science is further echoed in the call to focus on repeated processes and the concatenation of effects in various social scenarios. This perspective challenges the notion of deterministic social laws and instead promotes a more guarded understanding of how social outcomes are influenced by a web of interrelated factors and conditions. By emphasizing causal mechanisms and their interactions at multiple levels, this approach aligns with Hardin's view on the unpredictability and variability inherent in social systems. It underscores the importance of context and the specific configurations of elements that drive social phenomena, moving beyond a one-size-fits-all approach to understanding society. This shift toward recognizing the complexity and indeterminacy of social systems reflects a broader movement in political economy and philosophy, acknowledging the dynamic and multifaceted nature of societal interactions.

One may recognize in all these the major contours of the shift toward a context-focused approach. The message seems to be clear as it goes beyond simply issues related to the institutional design and feasibility analysis. We need to reconsider our approaches and theoretical ambitions, recognizing the centrality of a variety of elements difficult to account for in universal or grand-scale generalizable ways: historical, institutional, technological, psychological, cultural, demographic, ideological, and epistemological. When, where, in what settings, on what premises, under what conditions and circumstances, in what sequence, all these matter. Once we realize that to answer the big questions of social science, our reply is mostly invariably "it depends," we realize that a major rethinking of our epistemic objectives and parameters is required.

In brief: a consequence of the insights grown during the last couple of decades in the study of advanced capitalist and developing political economies, as supported by the NIE theoretical apparatus and analytics, gives some plausibility to the thesis that multiple institutional arrangements are compatible with development, that economic performance may be possible under a larger variance of institutional arrangements. In other words, economic performance may come in many institutional forms, and one of the goals of political economy should be to understand how the experience with the division of labor and markets is shaped by the unique institutional configurations under which it operates. The idea is that there may be a diversity of institutional arrangements leading to a diversity of economic systems, all compatible with some criteria of economic performance has thus been established as a legitimate conjecture.

2.3 Possibilism and the Feasibility Challenge

We have seen how, in the light of the "institutional diversity" reinforced by the "contextual" perspective, the strong conjecture that "there is no unique core of configurations of institutions associated structurally and functionally with economic performance" may be established. We have now a relatively in-depth understanding of the developments that made it plausible to think of a larger range of institutional configurations, of feasible economic systems, than the narrow band suggested by the classical comparative economic systems literature as reinforced by the 1989 evolutions. Thus we are now in the position to see why in many respects what Albert O. Hirschman calls "Possibilism" becomes a credible and legitimate way to define and articulate the emerging new vision.

Hirschman's concept of possibilism represents a clear departure from traditional deterministic views, emphasizing the potential for change and innovation within socio-economic systems, even under constraints or less-than-ideal conditions. The importance of human agency and creativity in overcoming obstacles is underscored, suggesting that individuals and groups in economic and social contexts can respond to challenges in resourceful ways. In this respect, in Hirschman's framework, possibilism is not just a philosophical stance but a practical tool that broadens the exploration of potential solutions and paths for progress. It highlights the significance of context in shaping possibilities and asserts that outcomes are not predetermined by structures or systems but are open to change through human action. Hence it carries an inherent optimism about the potential for positive change and encourages the exploration of a wide range of possibilities.

Hirschman's Possibilism extends beyond the recognition of human agency in economic and social contexts. It incorporates a nuanced understanding of how institutional settings and initial conditions influence the realm of possibilities. This perspective aligns with the complex interplay of variables in social systems, where outcomes are not solely the result of linear, deterministic processes but rather the culmination of various interacting elements (Room 2011) and with the volitional pragmatist approaches to social theory advanced by authors like Daniel Bromley (2006) or the emphasis on human agency and intentionality of old institutionalism.

Furthermore, possibilism, broadly defined, challenges the status quo of social science methodologies. It invites researchers to consider the unpredictability and adaptability of human behavior, emphasizing the importance of context and situational variables in shaping outcomes. This approach encourages an exploration of a broader spectrum of social phenomena, advocating for flexibility and openness in theoretical and empirical investigations. In doing so, it contributes significantly to the interface with social sciences, proposing an unorthodox portrayal of social dynamics and public policy.

But if that is the case, then the question becomes: Is there any way one could sort out from the endless combinatorial possibilities, ex ante, the feasible from the unfeasible? Is there a more general, theoretical way to make sense and separate the possible from the impossible and the feasible from the unfeasible, other than by trial and error? Given the high risks and tradeoffs involved in experimenting with human individuals, communities, and societies, shouldn't we be more guarded about such experimentation? Or, to be even more precise: Can the inherent optimism in possibilism lead to underestimating challenges or ignoring potential negative outcomes, thereby compromising realism in planning and decision-making? Given that structural constraints in society or economics can significantly limit agency and creativity, how does Hirschman's concept realistically address these limitations?

While possibilism encourages innovative and adaptive approaches to socioeconomic challenges, it also carries certain risks: For instance, radical reforms, change, or social experiments, implemented without sufficient understanding of potential consequences, could lead to unintended negative impacts on livelihoods, social structures, cultural norms, local economies, and social bonds. Engaging in experiments encouraged by possibilism comes with the risk of failure. Failure may have many causes, but one important cause may be avoided if the ex ante general feasibility is correctly assessed. Again, the stakes are high, as it is critical to avoid subjecting people to trials of systems that are not feasible. Implementing unfeasible systems can lead to significant social and economic costs, including wasted resources, disruption of communities, and potential harm to individuals' well-being.

How should we proceed in possibilist universes given the existence of feasibility sets? Could we consider an institutional arrangement by its very nature, irrespective of context, (un)feasible? Are there cases of institutional universal feasibility? Are there cases of universal institutional non-feasibility? If yes, how do we determine that? What is the relevance of such ideal, extreme cases? What are the criteria to be used to determine feasibility? What are the reasonable degrees of freedom we have in this respect? Even if we are unable to say what works with certainty, is it possible to say with certainty what doesn't work? These and many similar questions and challenges are thus raised by these developments brought to the fore by the institutionalist revolution and by the evolution of the associated research programs.

In the past, the socialist economic calculation debate was precisely about that: An investigation into what is feasible and what is not in comparative economic arrangements, an attempt to determine ex ante the feasibility space of alternative institutional designs and economic systems. Looking back, the bottom line is evident: One cannot simply engage in large-scale social experiments just on the assumption of possibilisms. It is not prudent to act only on the basis of a hope in the power of human agency and creativity in overcoming constraints. A strong belief that outcomes are not preordained by structures or systems, but rather are open to change through human action, comes with some challenges and risks. The economic calculation debate and the 100 years of socialist experimentation impacting millions and millions all over the globe are reminders in this respect. We need to integrate the lessons learned and the wealth of theoretical and historical knowledge as it has been shaped by the new institutional diversity and contextualist perspectives. How much more precisely should that take place? The rest of the volume will outline three venues, each contributing in its own way to the development of a more consistent epistemological, theoretical, methodological, and analytical basis for addressing these questions.

3 Institutional Structure and Performance: Comparative Economic Systems, Institutional Analysis, and the Endogenization of Feasibility

The previous section has identified and discussed the broad insights and conclusions of NIE and its underlying collective action research program regarding institutional diversity and the contextualization of institutional performance and institutional feasibility analysis. In this section, we will take a closer look at one possible way of using as a vehicle the traditional conceptual and analytical frameworks of comparative economic systems as a background for institutional analysis, in order to further articulate and organize these insights at the more granular level.

Our approach will use two basic frameworks, one based on comparative economic systems (Koopmans–Montias framework) and the other based on institutional theory (the Ostroms' Institutional Analysis and Development Framework). By situating NIE within the framework of comparative economic systems, we explore how new institutionalism has opened up a fresh perspective on social systems and policy studies. In other words, we will see again, from a different angle, how contextualism and possibilism emerge naturally from the institutionalist revolution by applying its research logic to the traditional elements concentrated on the economic systems and environmental variables. But at the same time, the section will take a step further in two ways. First, it will show how one may use these analytical frameworks not only to pinpoint and conceptualize the problem of feasibility but also to underscore the immense complexity of analyzing and predicting the viability of governance arrangements. Second, the section will show how an ingenious solution to the problem of feasibility, seen as an institutional epistemology problem, has emerged as a result of these developments: The endogenization of feasibility, redefining the search for feasibility as an integral part of a process of institutional adaptation and evolution.

3.1 The Comparative Economic Systems Framework

Given the fact that the type of problems at the core of our investigation has been mostly studied in the past by the field of comparative economic systems, we start with the well-established Comparative Economic Systems Koopmans–Montias framework as a first-order approach (Koopmans and Montias 1971). Conceptually, the economy is represented as a structure $\varepsilon = (e, s, ps, o)$, where the outcome o is a function of three variables: the environment (e), the economic system (s), and government policies within that system (ps). Additionally, it involved applying evaluative criteria (noted as "n" in their terms) to both quantitative and qualitative outcomes (o).

To give a general sense of the approach, let us briefly note that Koopmans and Montias describe "outcomes" as any aspect or consequence of a system via decisions, or actions of participants, to which value is assigned based on certain norms. Examples include per capita consumption levels, resource use efficiency, equitable living conditions or opportunities, and public service provision. These outcomes vary depending on factors like private/public property mix and centralized/decentralized control over production and consumption. The approach combined positive and normative analysis. Often, outcomes identify desirable aspects more strongly than systemic features or policies. Norms are evaluative functions applied to outcomes, representing preferences relevant to a comparison. There are two methods to construct them: ordinal and cardinal. Ordinally, a norm compares performance structures, with a relation R indicating that one economy has better outcomes than another, based on specific evaluative criteria. Cardinally, a norm assigns a value to economies, using a fixed value as a threshold to interpret acceptable outcomes. This dual approach allows for both structural-comparative and value-based assessments of economic performance.

We are now in a position to more accurately identify what the contextualist, NIE approach brings to the table, especially in comparison to the traditional CES framework, using a common language and logic. As noted, the CES framework characterizes an economy (ε) through three core components: the environment (e), the economic system (s), and the policy settings (ps). These components interact to produce various outcomes (o), which we then evaluate or compare using specific norms (n). The formula $n(o) = n[f(e, s, ps)]$ encapsulates this comparative-evaluative method, providing a structured approach to assessing and comparing different economic environments. Given the analytical structure above, the contextualist challenge comes from concentrating on the analytical effort of unpacking two key areas of interest: the economic system (s) and the environment (e) variables. Let us take them one by one.

We start with the "economic system." The first major difference is that in traditional comparative economic systems research, the analysis deals with two clusters of institutional features, one called capitalism and the other socialism. An economic system was indeed considered multidimensional, defined by its n attributes. It was also recognized that a system cannot be defined in terms of only one characteristic; multiple characteristics are necessary before its nature is specified. However, in practice, those characteristics were limited mainly to a set of two: property rights and mechanisms of coordination.

A two-by-two matrix was thus built. That was enough to create a typology for the entire population of possible economic systems under that framing. On one axis were placed the mechanisms of setting goals (such as plan vs. market) or principles of decision-making (such as centralization vs. decentralization). The other axis featured two types of property: private and public. The result was a set of four combinations, each configuration being associated with a label: capitalist, communist, market socialist, and fascist. These mechanisms/characteristics were seen operating in a very limited number of clusters and defining a homogenous institutional space at the level of something called the "national economy."

On the other hand, in the NIE approach, a more nuanced approach is implied. Again, the system is defined by a number of attributes, but they are more flexibly and diversely defined. A system is seen as a more diverse bundle of combinations that could take much more forms and at much more levels. A variety of clusters, based on a variety of possible combinations, on multiple dimensions, are taken into account. Second, even if these mechanisms/characteristics are seen as operating in clusters and necessary linkages, they are not seen as generating a homogenous institutional space. Multiple forms of arrangement create a heterogeneous space. For instance, private, public, and commons operate in a diverse mix in a "national economy." Different levels of aggregation of the characteristics are possible, from the basic operational level to the constitutional level (Ostrom 2005; Aligica and Boetke 2009).

In this respect, NIE goes not only beyond classical comparative economic systems but also beyond the Varieties of Capitalism (VoC) approach, sharing some key features with endogenous growth theory. For example, VoC examines market mechanisms, corporate governance, industrial relations, education and training, and interfirm relationships. New Institutional Economics extends its scope to more specific configurations, such as what the Ostroms refer to as "public economies" (Ostrom 1998). The notion of public economy, as defined by the Ostroms, challenges and transcends the conventional view that separates the market-based private sector from the government-driven public sector. Also, it cuts across the different standard functional forms and units. Instead, the public economy embodies a complex institutional architecture where markets, hierarchies, and a variety of hybrid arrangements coalesce. Coproduction, a key concept in this paradigm, highlights the collaborative efforts between government entities and citizens in producing and managing public goods and services. This approach not only redefines the structure and functioning of public sector activities beyond the typology of centralized bureaucratic systems but also introduces a nuanced understanding of governance where multiple centers of authority, competitive pressures, and cooperative arrangements drive efficiency and responsiveness to public needs.

For instance, within the framework of a public economy, one may illuminate how collective consumption units play a pivotal role. These units are essentially associations of individuals organized to articulate demand, share costs, and regulate the access and use of public goods and services, addressing challenges such as free-riding and strategic preference revelation. Within this context, the organization of production can vary significantly, involving a range of actors from governmental units to private and not-for-profit entities. This conceptualization transcends the state-market, public-private binary, and macro typologies of VoC, providing a deeper grasp of the diverse methods of producing, delivering, and consuming goods and services, underscoring the inherent flexibility and diversity of economic systems (Aligica and Tarko 2013). In brief, NIE redefines the terms in which institutional arrangements defining an economy or social system are seen and studied. With that, it provides a much more complex apparatus for analyzing the conditions of institutional performance as well as those of institutional feasibility.

When it comes to the "environment," the departure of NIE is even more drastic. In traditional comparative economic systems, the analysis was dealing with the environment mostly as a residual. It was mainly the result of a first-step heuristic and analytical need to isolate the impact of the system (s) on performance/outcomes (o), and in order to do that, one has to isolate and hold constant the environmental (e) and policy (p_s) variables. So, the treatment of the environment, in the function of analytical tasks and circumstances, was mixing more or less arbitrary factors pertaining to economic conjuncture/cycle, global trends, demographic and geopolitical factors, actions of other countries, natural resources, and so on factors, known stock of human and material resources, impact of weather, and even transitory tastes and preferences of the population.

New Institutional Economics deals with the "environment" aspect in two apparently contrasting ways, which in effect may be seen as parts of a two-step approach. The first is to simply expand it by systematically taking into account all possible factors determining institutional structure and performance. In other words, to focus on the specific institutional arrangement of interest and to start charting around it the main components of its operating environment. In many cases, that means to introduce elements related to multiple levels of analysis and multifaceted institutional forms. This more institutionally and functionally focused approach radically changes the very idea of what the "environment" is and how it should be conceptualized.

For instance, one aspect of the analysis might focus on the very institutional interactions within complex social systems seen as an environment for institutional structure and performance. As the number of institutions increases in a given space, their interactions intensify, significantly influencing the performance and resilience of each institution. The institutional ecology operates even at the pure quantitative level. But the qualitative differences are very relevant. These interactions can be horizontal (occurring at the same level) or vertical (spanning different levels) and have varying impacts, either strengthening or weakening the institutions involved. The nature of these interactions also ranges from symmetrical to asymmetrical, some being unidirectional and others increasingly reciprocal. The emergence of functional interdependencies and strategic links is inevitable in such interconnected fields, and they sheep at their turn the functional environment of the institutional forms.

The second step involves constructing robust frameworks designed to bring clarity and structure to the analysis of complex and often indeterminate interactions within social systems. Given the multifaceted nature of these systems, where countless variables interact in unpredictable ways, particularly across different levels of society (such as local, regional, national, and global), it becomes crucial to introduce order and identify patterns that can guide our understanding and decision-making processes.

Firstly, they help to systematically organize the various elements at play, allowing researchers and policymakers to better understand how the "environment" may be differently conceptualized at different levels. Changes at one level of the system may be seen as environmental changes for other levels. For example, a policy change at the national level might have cascading effects down to the local level, and vice versa. By focusing on the interplay across social levels, they represent a crucial step in moving from a chaotic, overwhelming landscape of possibilities to a more structured and actionable understanding of how social systems function and evolve (Young 2002). Again, NIE takes a much more systematic and careful look at what in CES was lumped under the (e) "environment" variable.

In this respect, we can take another step further, using as a reference point and guide E. Ostrom and her collaborators, who have elaborated in the context of the new institutionalism what they called the IAD framework (Ostrom 2005, 15). The Institutional Analysis and Development (IAD) framework is a comprehensive tool designed to dissect and understand the intricate interactions and outcomes that emerge within various institutional arrangements operating in different environments. As such, it's providing an approach to the problems of contextualism and possibilism via the methodical analysis of relationships between institutional arrangements and their operating environment.

3.2 The Institutional Analysis and Development (IAD) Framework

The IAD framework aims to capture and use for analytical and design purposes the pivotal role of rules, norms, and strategies in shaping the behavior of actors within any given institutional context. By providing a structured method for examining how these institutional arrangements influence decision-making processes, the IAD framework allows analysts to systematically explore how different designs affect the behavior of individuals and groups, leading to specific outcomes.

At its core, the IAD framework consists of three main components: the action arena, actors, and outcomes. It lays the groundwork for systematically investigating each relevant action arena, as well as its specific environment and outcomes. It involves a detailed mapping of different action arenas – distinct contexts where actors interact under specific rules and norms – along with the surrounding environmental factors that influence these interactions. Analyzing these arenas one by one allows for the reconstruction of complex clusters of institutional arrangements and processes that operate across various levels of society. This step-by-step approach provides a clear and comprehensive picture of how different institutional layers and their interactions contribute to overall system performance, offering insights into the dynamics that govern institutional effectiveness and adaptability.

In the context of our discussion, it is crucial to understand that this approach provides a valuable insight into the initiation of different "feasibility spaces" at various levels through manipulation of the meta-level rules of the game. Feasibility spaces refer to the range of options or actions that are possible within a given institutional or decision-making framework. When social actors operate at a meta-level – meaning they focus on the overarching rules and principles that govern the entire system – they are essentially shaping the boundaries within which decisions can be made and institutions can be designed in relation to specific "action arenas."

These multiple levels of structure, which are embedded within one another, create a complex and interconnected menu of choices, each making possible a different set of scenarios that may be or may not be actualized. Each level of rules or norms influences the options available at the subsequent level, thereby determining the feasibility of certain decisions or institutional designs. For instance, a change in the meta-level rules might expand or restrict the set of feasible actions at a lower level, thereby influencing the strategic choices available to actors within the system. This layered approach helps us understand how decisions made at a higher level of governance or policy can cascade down, altering the landscape of possibilities at more localized levels. By acknowledging the creation of these feasibility spaces, we gain a deeper understanding of the importance of considering not just immediate choices but also the foundational rules that shape and constrain those choices across different levels of the system.

Typical and illustrative for this approach is James Buchanan's distinction between pre-constitutional and post-constitutional choice and rules in his analysis of two stages of collective decision-making (Buchanan 2004). Pre-constitutional choice involves establishing the basic framework or "rules of the game" for a society, including the formation of institutions and the principles that govern collective action. It's about setting the foundational rules that determine how collective decisions will be made. Post-constitutional choice, on the other hand, occurs within the established framework and involves day-to-day decision-making and policy formation based on the rules set during the pre-constitutional stage. These decisions are about specific actions and policies within the existing constitutional framework.

Elinor and Vincent Ostrom build on Buchanan's constitutional political economy by extending its insights to a broader range of institutional arrangements. They operationalize Buchanan's distinction between three levels of rules: (a) constitutional, which sets foundational principles and constraints; (b) collective-choice, which defines how groups make policy decisions; and (c) operational, which guides day-to-day behavior. By clarifying how these layers interact, the Ostroms provide a framework for understanding governance dynamics, identifying leverage points, and improving institutional performance. The Ostroms show how understanding how different layers of rules function within a governance structure – specifically, high-level constitutional rules, collective-choice rules, and operational rules – significantly enhances our ability to navigate and manage the complexity and variability inherent in governance systems. This multitiered approach reveals how different combinations of rules at each level can operate with feasibility spaces via a wide array of institutional arrangements.

That brings us back to the core point of this argument: How the new institutional economic developments have brought to the fore the problem of institutional diversity and contextualized, and with it the twin problem of possibilism and the feasibility issue. By placing NIE developments on the background of CES frameworks, we have shown how NIE has offered the prospect of an alternative view of the institutional system. That view has, on the one hand, created the conditions for better identifying the contours of institutional feasibility and, at the same time, revealed the tremendous magnitude, complexity, and responsibility of the task of determining ex ante the feasibility of institutional and governance arrangements.

We are now in the position to understand more precisely how the diversity, contextuality, possibilism, and feasibility issues have emerged in a natural way by simply applying the underlying logic of the research program to two key elements of the traditional comparative economic systems formula: the "economic system" and the "environment" variables. But once the problem of institutional artifacts and the relationship between rules, incentives, and knowledge processes in the creation of those artifacts is conceptualized, the problem of feasibility spaces takes an interesting turn: from mostly an epistemic problem to one of institutional and social epistemology.

3.3 The Endogenization of Feasibility

The developments discussed so far represent more than just incremental advances in scientific knowledge through the addition of new variables. They also indicate a profound shift in methodological, theoretical, and epistemological perspectives, signaling a paradigmatic change in the way we approach the study of social systems. This shift has the potential to fundamentally alter our understanding of how social structures operate, how changes occur, and how we can manage prediction and control within these settings. Consequently, it directly impacts the broader issue of feasibility, which lies at the heart of applied theory and philosophy.

One of the most remarkable outcomes of the NIE noted earlier took place at the interface with the domain of social epistemology. Its trademark was an attempt to institutionally endogenize the questions of feasibility and institutional design. This approach suggests that instead of treating feasibility as an external constraint or a precondition that needs to be evaluated before implementing an institutional system, one may integrate the process of assessing and refining feasibility within the very operations of the institutional system itself.

In other words, the search for viable solutions should not be a separate, preliminary task (or post-factum retrospective assessment) but should be embedded in the ongoing functions and dynamics of the institutional system. As institutions evolve and operate, they continuously test and adapt their structures, rules, and processes in response to the realities they encounter. This self-referential process allows institutions to dynamically adjust to changing conditions, refining their feasibility in real-time rather than relying on static, predetermined criteria. By embedding the search for feasibility within the institution's normal functioning, this approach emphasizes a form of institutional self-correction and learning. It suggests that institutions are best understood as adaptive systems capable of evolving in response to internal and external challenges. The main policy active may be in these circumstances to ensure that the continuous process of adaptation remains viable and effective over time.

This shift in thinking has been significantly facilitated by the emergence and prominence of the concept of polycentric systems within institutional theory. Models of polycentric systems, characterized by multiple overlapping and competing decision centers and jurisdictions, have reshaped our understanding of institutional diversity. These systems, which allow for ongoing experimentation, adaptation, and tinkering, are ideally suited for continuously probing and adjusting the boundaries of feasibility and desirability. Each center or jurisdiction within a polycentric system can independently experiment with different approaches to governance and problem-solving. This diversity of approaches not only enhances the system's ability to adapt to local conditions and preferences but also creates a dynamic environment where successful strategies can be identified, shared, and potentially scaled across the broader system.

The idea is that polycentric systems act as a social coordination and search engine, where the collective process of trial, error, and learning across various jurisdictions continuously refines what is feasible and desirable (Gaus 2016; Müller 2019). The ongoing interactions and competitions between these jurisdictions ensure that institutional designs are not static but evolve in response to real-world challenges. Furthermore, by embedding the mechanisms for innovation and adaptation within the structure of the system itself, polycentricity ensures that institutions bolster that ability to tailor approaches to specific contexts while maintaining the capacity to evolve and remain flexible and responsive to changing circumstances.

A corollary of this perspective is that the concepts of what is desirable and what is feasible are continuously defined, redefined, calibrated, and tested through an ongoing process of experimentation and adaptation. The approach recognizes that both desirability and feasibility are context-dependent and subject to change as new information, technologies, and social dynamics emerge. Rather than adhering to a rigid set of criteria or standards, this process allows for the continuous exploration of possibilities, where ideas and strategies are regularly evaluated and adjusted in light of real-world outcomes and shifting conditions.

Consequently, governance and public policy are not seen merely as targeted interventions aimed at modifying specific variables within a fixed system. By prioritizing the conditions that enable continuous adjustment and learning, this model of governance supports the constant reevaluation of what is just and feasible, allowing for more nuanced and contextually appropriate responses to complex social challenges. It is a process-oriented perspective that values adaptability and resilience, recognizing that sustainable and effective governance must evolve alongside the society it seeks to serve: "a framework in which different perspectives can search, share, debate, and dismiss each other's insights, while engaging in cooperative social relationships (Gaus 2016, 243)."

The process perspective shifts the focus from an ideal, a final state or goal, to the decentralized activity and the interaction between social actors (Barry 1988). That is to say, the goal is not to establish a fixed, ideal state but rather to develop a set of rules and guiding principles that allow for flexibility and adaptability within the system. These rules should be designed to evolve in response to changes in the environment and shifts in the preferences of social actors, ensuring that the system remains relevant and effective over time. One could see easily why that implies a polycentric system characterized by institutional diversity and ongoing experimentation, an approach that transcends traditional models of intervention by incorporating multiple levels of analysis and action into the process of institutional change, design, and feasibility.

To sum up, once the institutionalist approach to feasibility it followed to its ultimate implications, it leads to a vision of a social-epistemic framework that blends incentives with the active elicitation and mobilization of knowledge. This approach is grounded in the notion that what is ideal and what is feasible should not be treated as static concepts but rather as dynamic realities that are continually explored, tested, and refined. Through a diversity of collective and interactive arrangements, institutions and social actors engage in a process of constant experimentation and adjustment. The boundaries of ideals – whether they pertain to justice or practical implementation – are regularly probed, reconfigured, and fine-tuned in response to ongoing learning and real-world feedback. This approach emphasizes the importance of "tinkering in the neighborhood," meaning that solutions and improvements are sought incrementally, in close proximity to existing practices, allowing for gradual but meaningful progress toward better institutional outcomes.

Institutional epistemology combines two key elements: The first is given by the institutional processes (as framed by the institutional structures). The second is the quality of the epistemic input provided by human agents. The agents initiate, manage, and oversee these processes using their capabilities and judgment. While this institutional epistemology approach helps reduce some of the cognitive and decision-making burden on individuals, it does not eliminate it entirely. Individuals still bear the responsibility for developing criteria, gathering observations, collecting and filtering data about these processes, using their judgment.

So, in the end, the task of developing methods and heuristics to help human judgment assess the feasibility set – what lies within the space of the possible and feasible, what lies outside, and how the boundary between the two shifts under different conditions – remains stringent. These challenges are complex, and the institutionally embedded, empirically experiential approach can only take us so far in addressing them.

3.4 Conclusions

One of the consequences of the institutionalist research program is a new perspective, which, among others, encourages us to think in terms of a social-epistemological endogenization of the feasibility issue. Whether this is the ultimate implication of the institutionalist revolution – an implication of paradigmatic change proportions – or it is simply seen as just a stronger version of an already well-acknowledged insight recognizing the epistemic and social adaptation properties of systems based on the flexibility induced by democratic and market economy principles, is a separate discussion.

That being said, a problem remains. At a closer look, the endogenization of the search process (or the social epistemology of the social search of the ideal in a nonideal world) doesn't seem to be fully "the solution" one expects it to be. Even in such a polycentric, knowledge process, and experimentation-based social system in which a bottom-up process of institutional search and adaptation is shaping the creation, change, and demise of institutional arrangements, the problem of institutional feasibility remains. It is only that the accent has then shifted. In itself, the challenges of identifying the feasibility set continue to exist. We have just simply passed it on, declining responsibility while claiming "let people decide" as part of the social and institutional games and processes they set up and participate in. However, for the players on the ground, for those directly involved in institutional design and institutional experimentation, the problem remains as stringent. Is it possible to determine the range of the feasibility set ex ante?

When confronted with these endless combinatorial possibilities, the question becomes: Is there a more general, theoretical way to make sense of and separate the possible from the impossible and the feasible from the unfeasible, other than by trial and error? How do we determine that? How do we draw the line between the viable combinations and the less viable ones? It is crucial to identify heuristics and conceptual and theoretical criteria to be used in order to weed out (eliminate) unfeasible alternatives. One needs, at minimum, a basic negative strategy of identifying the unfeasible.

Creating taxonomies and correlating them with performance indices may provide some indications of what was historically possible and feasible. But, obviously, the problem of external validity looms large. One likes it or not, but the deep philosophical problems of levels of generalization, social ontology, possible worlds, scenarios thinking, natural kinds, extrapolation, probabilities, induction, and so on loom large and force us to go beyond the boundary of positive empirical analysis. Hence a meta-level approach is required that implies looking at concrete case studies in feasibility analysis in conjunction with the discussion of the conceptual/theoretical conditions for the feasibility set (exploring how the logic of combinations maps on the feasible) as well as of the philosophical and logical foundation of our thinking on these lines. The next two sections will provide two excursions into these two different but complementary directions.

4 The Economic Calculation Debate Revisited: Exchange, Rivalry, and Institutions

The previous section used frameworks based on comparative economic systems and institutional theory as its foundation. This section shifts the approach. Instead of starting with theoretical frameworks, it begins with a specific problem: the problem of economic calculation. Regardless of the angle of approach or conceptual apparatus, any discussion about the feasibility of institutional arrangements ultimately centers on the issues of incentives, information, and the efficacy of allocating efforts and resources. In other words, tackling the problem traditionally known as the "economic calculation problem" is unavoidable.

Focusing on the challenge of economic calculation as a feasibility issue allows us to revisit the lessons and insights, as well as the compounded theoretical instruments, that grew over the past century in the debates surrounding this problem. This will enable us to open an alternative perspective on the institutional epistemology processes discussed in the previous section, and explore how some of their facets, as illustrated by the theoretical corpus have developed, in response to this debate, particularly within the tradition of the Austrian School of Economics. As the section is going to show, the integrated vision that has emerged allows us to analyze feasibility within a theoretical model that combines three interrelated elements: conflict theory (rivalry), institutional theory (rules of the game), and knowledge process theory (price systems). Conflict theory emphasizes the importance of competition; institutional theory focuses on how institutions channel this competition productively; and knowledge process theory emphasizes the role of prices in facilitating economic coordination. Together, these elements create a theoretically informed and empirically relevant understanding of the nature and dynamics of a market process and of the feasibility issue in connection to economic calculation.

4.1 The Communist Experiment and the Feasibility Issue

By all accounts, communism as a historical phenomenon defining the twentieth century can be viewed as a grand social experiment unparalleled in human history. That involved radical changes in governance, economic structures, and social relations, significantly affecting millions and influencing the course of modern history. The scale and impact of communism (be it presented under this label or as "socialism") are difficult to overestimate. The period of communist grand revolutionary experiments spans over a century. The 1917 Bolshevik Revolution in Russia marked the inception of the first major communist state, which later expanded into various forms across different countries, notably Eastern Europe, China, and parts of Southeast Asia and Latin America. The peak of this era was during the mid twentieth century, characterized by the Cold War between the capitalist West and the communist East when communism was a truly global phenomenon. The late twentieth century, particularly the 1980s and 1990s, witnessed significant decline. Today, its legacy and influence continue to impact global politics, the climate of opinion, and socio-economic structures.

The experience of communist states provides a unique perspective on the complexities of large-scale social engineering, highlighting the challenges and consequences of attempting radical socio-economic transformations. As such, it serves as a crucial case study in the desirability and feasibility of governance systems and institutional arrangements. The case is a repository of profound insights helping our understanding of governance, economic systems and social change, and the practical limits of political and economic theories.

For the purposes of our discussion, it is important to recognize that even before the implementation of communist-socialist systems in real life, there was a major controversy about their feasibility. Today, seen in retrospect, it may legitimately be considered the most important debate in the intellectual history of modern social sciences and social philosophy. The controversy delved into the structure and function of this type of system, questioning its realizability in light of not only the technological and social conditions at the start of the twentieth century but also considering intrinsic universal aspects of human nature and social ontology. As such, it is one of the most important sources of insights regarding of social change and institutional feasibility.

From the perspective of our study, the most significant aspect comes from the fact that the debate was not about the desirability of socialism, but about its feasibility. The issue of desirability is defined by questions such as: Is the system inherently valuable, providing intrinsic benefits? Does it align with the deeper aspirations and ethical ideals of the society it aims to govern? How does the system contribute to the development and flourishing of human capabilities and individual's potential? Those skeptical about socialism accepted to take desirability for granted. In other words, they accepted that a system broadly defined by the socialist blueprint was desirable. They framed thus the debate in the following terms: Presuming that socialism/communism as a system is desirable, is it going to work as desired? Is a transformation from the current state of the economy and society to such a system, feasible?

And thus, avoiding the complex issues of desirability, it concentrated the attention on feasibility, seen as a means-ends problem. The argument runs as follows: The end-goal is the establishment of a socialist system. The means to achieve this end involve designing and implementing institutional structures and economic processes that are intended to create and sustain the socialist system and ensure its effective performance. The question is: How effective are these institutional designs going to be in achieving the socialist end-goal?

Using the operational definition of socialism as a means-ends relationship, we can formulate the problem as follows: Do the means (institutional designs) align with and support the functioning and long-term success of the intended socialist end-goals? How effective are these institutional designs in realistically achieving the end-goals of a socialist system? Are the institutional designs proposed for achieving socialism practical in the current socio-economic and political contexts?

The most notable aspect is that, in addressing these questions, the debate on the feasibility of socialism focused on a single crucial aspect: the feasibility of economic calculation within a socialist framework. Instead of looking at the multitude of institutional arrangements, organizations, policies, economic processes, and governance mechanisms of the communist designs, and instead of getting dissipated and confused by the rhetorical and ideological presentation of those, it concentrated all the questions into one. That question addressed the crucial problem on which the entire edifice of the communist economy – and by implication of the entire communist system – depended: the rational allocation of resources based on the rational economic calculation. This topic became the defining feature of the discussion regarding the feasibility of socialism, the name under which it entered into history: the economic calculation problem, the problem of whether a socialist economy could effectively function and allocate resources.

During these heated exchanges on the feasibility of economic calculation in socialism and, by implication, about the feasibility of socialism itself, the foundation of modern thinking regarding comparative institutional analysis and institutional design was formulated, and the directions for the next 100 years of investigations and political economy, institutional theory, and comparative economic systems were set up. In brief, the debate not only fully articulated and challenged existing ideas but also set the stage for future explorations into how economic and political institutions could be designed and function effectively within various systems. As we are going to see, it is as relevant today, in its new avatars, as it was 100 years ago.

4.2 The Economic Calculation Debate: An Overview

In outlining the main aspects of the debate, we are going to follow the account given by Boettke et al. (2014). The account focuses not so much on a closely reconstructed intellectual history account, as on the underlying logic of the arguments exchanged and their evolution in time as a sequence of stages.

Initially, socialists, in their critique of capitalism, denied the relevance of economic analysis in a socialist society. They assumed that the laws of production and distribution could be a direct function of political will, neglecting the usual economic considerations and constraints. However, economists like Friedrich von Wieser, Leon Walras, Vilfredo Pareto, Enrico Barone, Fredrick Taylor, and Frank Knight argued that socialism would need to meet the same formal efficiency criteria as capitalism. Decisive for the dynamics of the debate was however Ludwig von Mises, who in his 1920 work "Economic Calculation in the Socialist Commonwealth," took the argument to its ultimate implications and made forcefully the point that economic calculation in socialism was necessary but intrinsically impossible.

Mises noted that socialism entails abolishing private property in production means and aims to transition from "necessity" to "freedom" by achieving advanced material production. But he drew attention to the fact that production nonetheless requires a rational use of resources. He questioned how socialism, without a private ownership system, market-established prices, and profit and loss accounting, could motivate and inform its participants to achieve this goal, arguing that the means of abolishing private property were incompatible with the end of advanced material production. Without private property in the means of production, he claimed, there would be no market for them, leading to a lack of money prices and an inability for planners to assess opportunity costs. This lack of economic guidance in a socialist system, he contended, would render rational resource allocation impossible, turning economic activity into a blind endeavor. Thus, Mises concluded that a "socialist economy" was an oxymoron, suggesting that socialism would result in planned chaos rather than a functional economy.

From 1920 to 1935, the debate on socialism was dominated by the Mises critique, with no counterargument gaining consensus among economists. But as Boettke et al. (2014) note, the Great Depression shook faith in capitalism's efficiency. Socialism started to be viewed as a promising alternative. More importantly, an article by Oskar Lange (Lange 1936, 1937) responding to Mises, garnered significant support among economists, leading to a consensus from 1937 to 1985 that the Austrian argument against socialism was defeated. Socialism had to be feasible. The table turned again in 1989. At that point, the historical and empirical evidence was strongly speaking against the feasibility or even the desirability of a socialist economic and social order. Thus, after 1989, things changed in a radical way, and the Austrian victory was proclaimed. A short-lived victory, only to be again questioned by a new wave of skepticism regarding the merit of the argument after 2008 in the aftermath of the financial crisis and the IT revolution.

Before moving ahead, let's note that the problem of feasibility remains equally relevant irrespective of the side winning the debate. As Benjamin Ward noted, at the "heart" of the socialist controversy is the question: "Can a socialist society find some method of organizing the allocation of resources which will permit the economy to function with a tolerable degree of efficiency?" (Ward 1967, 3–4). Reviewing the debate, he concludes that "many, perhaps most, economists would consider it established that the appropriate answer is 'yes.'" But then he adds immediately that the question should, however, be considered still open. The reason is the existence of a "variety of conceivable forms of socialist economy." Hence the answer "may not be 'yes' for every one of these." In other words, the economic calculation debate provides a benchmark for the discussions regarding feasibility and its limits. The problem of feasibility and their application of the logic of the possible and viable remain valid irrespective of which side has the upper hand in the theoretical debate.

Returning to the theoretical substance of that debate, as Boettke et al. (2014) explain, it is important to note that Lange refuted Mises by applying neoclassical economics to socialism; in order to be able to do that, he had to make a full turn into institutional theory territory. Lange's institutional design for socialism allowed a market for consumer goods and labor, with state control over production guided by strict efficiency criteria. Within this framework, Lange argued that socialism could theoretically match capitalist efficiency and even surpass it by eliminating monopolies and business cycles. His use of neoclassical theory, which Mises had relied on, was what turned the argument in favor of socialism's feasibility in the eyes of many economists. More precisely, Lange proposed a system where state-owned firms operate under neoclassical microeconomic principles, setting output where marginal cost equals price and ensuring production at minimum average cost. This system, theoretically, would use market signals, such as inventory levels, for trial-and-error adjustments, ensuring resource allocation efficiency (Boettke et al. 2014; Boettke 2015b).

The next stage of the debate came with Hayek's response to Lange's market socialism model. Hayek (1937, 1945, 1998) emphasized the need for market signals to coordinate production plans with consumer demands, arguing that this process is complex and cannot be simplified as in general equilibrium models. He made a step in the direction of realism. Hayek maintained that the process of coordination in a real market cannot be assumed away, as done in theoretical models. The focus on a state of equilibrium in economic models, he argued, overlooked the dynamic process of adaptation to changing circumstances. In fact, equilibrium-based models are irrelevant when confronted with real-world conditions where data and contexts are constantly evolving. Not the ideal and the end state of the equilibrium are the keys, but the processes are endlessly pushing in the direction of equilibrium.

But even more importantly, the Hayek approach set up a shift of focus in an attempt to bring to the foreground the real driver of analysis, which was not neoclassical equilibrium theory but the institutional parameters of equilibrating processes. From this perspective, calculation was not to be seen as an accounting or computational problem primarily. It was to be seen as an institutional one. His central argument was that without institutions like private property and mechanisms like price signals and profit/loss accounting – all absent in socialism – the necessary coordination of consumer and producer goods' value wouldn't occur. In other words, he prepared the way for an institutionalist turn in the debate, doubled by a knowledge and information theory turn.

When talking about a competitive environment, we are talking ultimately of structures and mechanisms of an institutional nature. But at the same time, we have to introduce a process view of things. Hayek argued that in competition, entrepreneurs must continuously discover the least-cost production methods and how to meet consumer demands. Effective resource allocation requires alignment between underlying conditions (tastes, technology, and resources) and market variables (prices and profit/loss). Perfect competition assumes complete alignment, eliminating coordination issues. But Hayek emphasized the lag between underlying economic conditions and market responses and the process this gap sets into motion and fuels. Claiming the mantle of a more realistic perspective and viewing economics as a science of tendencies and directions, he opened up the view of the market not as a model of formal equilibrium but as a process. Changes in fundamental conditions trigger market adjustments, with the market process gradually operating to align with these changes.

The difference between his approach and Lange's neoclassical view, where competition and market efficiency are static concepts, is significant. For Hayek, competition is a process, an intrinsic feature of complex phenomena in dynamics. The complex system prices not only denote exchange ratios but also play a vital role in economizing and conveying information and setting into motion an error-correcting social mechanism, a viewpoint differing from the interpretation offered by the neoclassical framework. The market is a self-correcting complex system that adjusts ongoingly the coordination of its apparatus with signals used as part of an intricate feedback system.

Only in this context can one understand the circumstances in which learning and knowledge processes become central. As Hayek argues, the perfect information assumption of the neoclassical mainstream was not only unrealistic but also analytically distorting. Thus, Hayek emphasized that perfect knowledge is characteristic of an equilibrium state but cannot be presumed in the equilibration process. In "Economics and Knowledge" (1937) and "The Use of Knowledge in Society" (1945), Hayek articulated an original take on the problem of information in economic analysis. He drew attention to two aspects of huge but neglected importance: (a) prices translate subjective trade-offs into objective information for market participants, while (b) knowledge in the market has a contextual nature, which implies that local, contextual knowledge is crucial for market participants and cannot be effectively utilized by planners for large-scale societal organization. Therefore, how economic agents learn is key to economics. The role of price signals in this learning process is essential. The process associated with learning in relationship with institutionally induced flows of information and knowledge gives a different take on the economic calculation problem.

With that, Hayek redefined the terms of the debate. By the 1950s, the institutionalist and information and knowledge process theory dimensions of the economic calculation issue were fully spelled out. The magnitude and profundity of his contribution had nonetheless to wait until 1989 to be recognized in all its applied-level implications. Yet after his contribution in the mid twentieth century, it became clear that the real economic calculation debate was not anymore about systems of equations and equilibrium models but about social and knowledge processes and the institutional structures associated with them.

4.3 The Debate: First Order Observations

Seen in the light of Boettke et al. (2014) and Lavoie (1985) all these were contributions to a broader understanding of the problems of the possibility and feasibility of economic and governance systems in general. The major point is this: While the discussions around the economic calculation debate may be seen as a series of observations on how the perception of victory in the debate has shifted over time, the crux of the matter lies deeper, in the theoretical frameworks of the intellectual tools and approaches underpinning the debate.

First of all, as we have seen, the debate highlighted a fundamental difference regarding the role of equilibrium in theory about these issues. On the one hand, there were those who viewed economic theory primarily as equilibrium theory, a perspective often implicit in neoclassical discussions of the calculation debate. For Mises and the Austrians, "economic theory" encompasses more than just equilibrium analysis. The static description may be useful analytically as a general starting point, but the primary concern is the system's dynamical equilibrating tendencies. Thus, for socialism to be economically viable, it must demonstrate that socialist institutions can replicate a form of dynamic equilibration, even without private capital ownership and other despised capitalist institutional forms. The focus is thus on the institutional arrangements and on the processes set into motion and governed by them.

To summarize, the Austrian economists brought forth in the debate an alternative perspective that was broader, deeper, and fundamentally different from the prevailing ones. This perspective significantly shifted the center of gravity of investigations and discussions when it comes to the feasibility of economic systems from formal projections and theoretical scenarios, to social theory. By offering this innovative viewpoint, the Austrians expanded the intellectual territory, pushing the debate into new realms in which social and process theorizing go way beyond the standard neoclassical economics. They prepared the way for a more realistic integration of the institutional element in their approach, which opened the door for a knowledge-process-based interpretation of information theory. Neoclassical formalism analytics and information theory have a role, but they have to be encapsulated in a social theory framework. This reorientation in thinking created fresh avenues for approaching economic phenomena as well as the possibility of advancing our understanding of the problem of the feasibility of various economic systems and institutional arrangements.

To be more precise, there are three focal points the Austrian theory authors advanced. The first is related to the structure and functioning of institutions within an economy, analyzing how they impact economic processes and outcomes. The second concentrates on countervailing forces and rivalry, examines the role of competition and opposing forces within the economic system, and how they contribute to the dynamism and evolution of economic structures. The third is related to information and knowledge processes, that is, the creation, flow, and utilization of information and knowledge within the economy, exploring how these elements drive economic decision-making and efficiency.

All of the above contribute to the theoretical scaffolding reshaping the ways we are thinking about the problem of institutional feasibility in the aftermath (and in the light) of the economic calculation debate. Let's take now a closer look at how they intertwined and supported each other, creating a unique theoretical framework for the analysis of the feasibility of institutional and governance structures involving or requiring economic calculation, and by extension of a variety of institutional and governance structures used in the modern world.

4.4 The Institutional Turn

The evolution of the economic calculation debate has led, in a natural way, to the problem of institutions (Boettke et al. 2014). The structure of prices and incentives that sets into motion the economic calculation process is ultimately a function of the underlying institutional arrangements. Various configurations of productive and allocative processes may be generated by different institutional configurations. Things that might be possible assuming a certain institutional configuration might not be possible if those assumptions are changed. That interpretation is far from singular. In fact, sooner or later even the hard-core neoclassical perspective comes down to do this. The scholars studying and following the evolution of the economic calculation debate from perspectives that are different from the Austrian ones have reached similar conclusions.

For instance, G. Hodgson (2016) advances a similar reading, saying that in his view both sides of the debate have missed the crucial relevance of institutions. Although the Austrians effectively challenged comprehensive central planning and won the debate, their approach failed to elaborate the institutional infrastructure behind general principles like privatization, competition, deregulation, and limiting state power. This approach, noted Hodgson, ironically mirrors the Marxists' omission, revealing an unexpected commonality between the two schools of thought.

In Hodgson's reading, the institutional dimension is in fact the real factor shaping the problem of feasibility. But in the twentieth-century capitalism versus socialism debate, both sides overlooked precisely that aspect and failed to accurately identify, specify, and define their respective systems. Socialism advocates relied on generic equilibrium models, neglecting the specific institutional details of both systems. Meanwhile, the Austrian school's definitions of private property and exchange were a move in the right direction, but they were too broad, lacking historical specificity, and failing to capture the unique institutional features of a market economy (Hodgson 2015). That being said, notes Hodgson, despite their failure to thoroughly address the necessary institutional structures for upholding property, exchange, and market systems, Mises and Hayek emphasized private property and markets as key solutions to economic issues, offering a more nuanced institutional perspective than their socialist counterparts (Hodgson 2016).

Summing up, a more nuanced interpretation of the aftermath of the debate and its legacy would identify several stages in the evolution of the Austrian perspective, the main bearer and the defining force framing the debate: The first stage in which the difference between, on the one hand, the mainstream neoclassical approach focused on equilibrium and, on the other hand, the approach focused on the market process is worked out. Then, based on that, an institutionalist turn is set into motion, constituting a second stage. The institutionalist turn heralded and already set up by Hayek becomes even more salient and robust in the next generation of Austrian theorists, out of which Peter Boettke is the most important contributor to this turn.

Boettke extensively elaborates multiple converging and complementing angles on the thesis that the underlying institutions of a society, give rise to the observed pattern of social cooperation discussed in the economic calculation debate. Under secure private property rights, individuals pursue productive opportunities and contribute to the process of economic development. The failed experiments of socialism are crucial case studies offering overwhelming empirical evidence in that respect (Boettke et al. 2014; Boettke 2015a).

In developing these arguments, Boettke followed otherwise the standard framework of comparative economic systems analytics. Institutions, explains Boettke, comprise "the basic rules of society to which its members adhere when interacting with one another." These are not to be confused with the policies that are pursued within the existing system of institutions. Whereas "variation in policies gives rise to short-run fluctuations in economic activity, it is the basic institutions that determine the long-run economic performance of a society" (Boettke and Fink 2011, 8). Because of the role of institutions as the "rules of the game," a detailed examination of the institutional context is crucial (Boettke and Coyne 2009).

With that – and similar observations and studies of the failure of socialism and the transition in Eastern Europe – it becomes evident that the crux of the problem of feasibility was moved into the sphere of institutional theory and analysis. This integration in the territory of institutionalism signifies that feasibility, as conceptualized in the Austrian tradition of economic thought, begins to align with the broader elements found in the broader trends of institutionalist literature, as surveyed in the previous section.

This convergence, very relevant for all the investigations regarding the feasibility issue, is both good and bad news. The reason is due to the fact that, as we have seen, embracing institutionalism includes embracing the twin challenges of institutional diversity and contextualism. As discussed, institutional diversity refers to the variety and complexity of institutional arrangements and their differing impacts on economic outcomes. Contextualism, on the other hand, emphasizes the importance of understanding these institutions within their specific historical, cultural, and situational contexts. Both aspects are crucial in analyzing feasibility. It means that feasibility analysis and design, from the perspective of Austrian institutionalism, has now to share many similarities – in assumptions, implications, and key themes – with other forms of institutionalism, despite their different origins and emphases.

That being said, there is nonetheless at least one specific theoretical and analytical dimension emerging of the economic calculation problem, which seems to be uniquely Austrian. Following the logic of Mises' argument leads not just to the institutional level. Pushed forward, toward the social foundations, in a surprising move, it engages the very problem of rivalry and conflict as a foundation of a social order in which the complex system of price signals, coordination, and rational allocation of resources is emerging. The result is an integrated view of the problem of feasibility, which unites the three domains (institutional theory, conflict theory, and theory of information and knowledge) into one framework.

4.5 Rivalry: Insights and Implications

Crucial for this move toward integrating conflict theory into the Austrian framework is Don Lavoie's work on rivalry and central planning (Lavoie 1985). Lavoie's work illustrates in a perhaps surprising way how rivalry and conflict are fundamental to the functioning of a social order, particularly in the context of economic systems. The "natural harmonies" of the "invisible hand" manifested in the market prices are the other facet of the tensions associated with rivalry and (institutionally structured) conflict. The two facets are intrinsically connected.

His analysis suggests that conflict-related elements are not merely disruptive forces but can be foundational to the emergence of a coordinated and rational economic system, primarily through the mechanisms of price signals. This groundbreaking insight is already present in Mises' work and his insistence on the role of competition. Don Lavoie takes this insight to the next level and makes a huge step toward fully articulating the three pillars of the Austrian theory as applied to the feasibility issue.

The core idea is this: The inherent rivalry and conflicts within economic systems play a crucial role in the process of generating the information and knowledge necessary for efficient economic decision-making. In Lavoie's analysis, the role of price signals remains central. Price signals, emerging from the interactions within a competitive market, provide the necessary information for the rational allocation of resources, guiding economic actors in their decision-making processes. However, there is another layer of social processes that needs to be unveiled. The layer of conflict, competition, and zero-sum games. By integrating institutional theory, conflict theory, and information-and-knowledge theory, this compounded theoretical perspective offers a comprehensive understanding of how economic systems function and adapt. It does that by bringing to the picture the missing link: the critical importance of rivalry and conflict in shaping the economic order, while challenging the conventional view that these elements are exclusively negative or disruptive.

Interestingly enough, G. Hodgson (2016) articulates again this intuition, following the implications of the logic of economic calculation debate, taken to the next level. Again, he is half right in his criticism, which notes that both the Austrian school and other participants in the socialist calculation debates often overlooked the significance of the role of counterbalancing processes in capitalism. But, as we have seen, that is precisely the point made by Don Lavoie's *Rivalry and Central Planning* (1985), and this is the point further elaborated by Boettke and his research program, which integrates the rivalry element in an institutionalist framework. A brief look at Lavoie's argument will help us to see the implications for the feasibility issue. In his book, Lavoie revisits and conceptually reconstructs the crucial debate over the possibility of economic calculation in socialism and, by implication, the very feasibility of organizing an economic system on socialist principles and central planning institutional designs.

Lavoie puts at the center of the Austrian approach the notion of economic rivalry defined as "the clash of human purposes, the aspect of the market relation revealed every time when market participants bid away resources from another" (Lavoie 1985, 22). The paramount question of the economic calculation debate, explains Lavoie, was which economic system is best for the following two objectives: (a) allocating resources to their most desired places, and (b) discovering the most efficient ways of production. The two leading contenders were the rivalrous competition of capitalism and the conscious planning of socialism. The determination of success was gauged by which system could better discover the appropriate knowledge that enables these goals.

The Austrians, as interpreted by Lavoie, made three claims in their defense of capitalism. First, the economic calculation inherent to capitalism allows entrepreneurs to "eliminate from consideration the innumerable possibilities of technologically feasible but uneconomic production processes" (Lavoie 1985, 57). Second, through the bidding away of resources from each other, the rivalrous competition of producers allocates resources to their most demanded employments. Finally, the Austrians claimed that socialism cannot retain or improve the technological productivity of capitalism. Lavoie further demonstrates that all these claims are dependent on rivalrous competition, which is institutionally interwoven, through the signaling and incentivizing functions of the price system, at the center of the market process.

Lavoie shows that both schools of the debate accepted rivalry as something present in competitive markets, but widely disagreed on its function. For Karl Marx, rivalry represented the discoordination of production plans. Resources are wasted in the capitalist production. By creating a central planning board, the socialists could eliminate this profligate rivalry. Ludwig von Mises, on the other hand, saw the function of rivalry as unearthing the knowledge that makes (a) the allocation of resources to their most desired places and (b) the most efficient way of production possible. Thus, revisiting and reconstructing conceptually the Austrian position, Lavoie finds rivalry center stage, vital to the mechanisms associated with capitalism and its economic performance.

Another way to put it is to say that rivalry is the phenomenon setting into motion a series of developments that, cumulated around the social exchange, come to create and fuel the market process. If socialism means abolishing rivalry and the institutions related to it, then socialism will not be able to allocate rationally its resources. Socialism will not be able to solve the economic calculation problem.

In brief, Lavoie placed the concept of conflict via rivalry at the basis of the Austrian approach and made it essential to any economic and social theory aiming at explaining the market process and the feasibility of alternatives to it, such as central planning and socialism. Indeed, Lavoie was able to show how both *exchange* and *rivalry* are key factors setting into motion the chain of processes that we associate with the functioning and structure of the market order, while at the same time, they are decisive for the understanding of the limits and of the feasibility of socialist institutional designs.

4.6 Rivalry, Exchange, and Institutional Structures

The focus on rivalry and the recognition of its significance alters in profound ways not only the way the Austrian theory is perceived but also our understanding of the feasibility issue. Austrian theory may now be seen not only as an unadulterated theory of coordination and cooperation, the mere inheritor of the "invisible hand" and "natural harmony" traditions, but also, and quite intriguingly, as a perspective that integrates significant aspects of conflict theory. Similarly, the feasibility issue, as reframed, may be considered more as a mere set of calculation issues, information process management, and optimizing rationality puzzles. The neo-Austrian theory is pointing beyond economic theory toward a broader social theory having a compounded theoretical apparatus with multiple building blocks and facets.

The apparatus captures the dual aspect of market mechanisms, illustrating both competitive and cooperative elements behind economic processes and transactions. On one hand, there's a zero-sum aspect where competition among entrepreneurs is emphasized. In this scenario, when producers successfully engage in a transaction, they "win" while another who fails to be part of it "loses." As we have seen, this competitive element is vital as it helps to reveal the true social value of resources. Entrepreneurs bid against each other for production inputs, indicating their willingness to pay. This rivalry is essential for determining the most valued use of each resource, as it uncovers the highest marginal product placement of these resources. Without such competition, it would be a real challenge to ascertain the true value and optimal allocation of resources.

On the other hand, the argument also points to a cooperative aspect, described as a win-win exchange. In this facet, the focus is on the mutual benefits derived from transactions. Each party in a transaction participates because they perceive a relative advantage based on their unique preferences and information. This is where the exchange of goods or services isn't about winning or losing but about mutual gain (Sugden 2020). This aspect emphasizes that, although competition is a driving force in market dynamics, the end-goal of transactions is cooperative, aiming for a mutually beneficial exchange between the parties involved.

It is evident that the discussion can be more precisely restated by explicitly highlighting the relationship between rivalry and price formation via institutional structures. This is actually the move that transcends pure economic theory and pushes into the boundary territories of social theory. It becomes clear upon closer examination that the emergence of prices and price systems, as aggregated phenomena, depends on both the supply-demand exchange aspect and the rivalry situation. Focusing solely on the supply-demand dynamic can obscure the role of rivalry as a major source of the knowledge process and the ensuing coordination patterns.

To sum up: institutional conditions play a pivotal role in shaping the economic landscape, particularly in terms of fostering competition and generating crucial market knowledge. These conditions, closely tied to specific exchange mechanisms, create an environment where rivalry among entrepreneurs becomes an orderly rivalrous bidding, while the competitive pressures channel the processes in productive directions. By setting rules and norms, institutions direct what could be destructive social conflict into a form of controlled competition that ultimately benefits the economy.

Within this space of rivalry and exchange, information is a critical component to be transformed into knowledge for informed decision-making. Information is not only discovered but also created. Then it is converted into actionable knowledge. That very allocation of resources refuels the process, which creates continuously new sets of information and knowledge, which motivates and shapes a new cycle of decisions and actions.

In brief, if the market is seen as a knowledge process, then the knowledge produced through the market has to be seen as anchored and depending on rivalry processes. This is without any doubt an exemplary case of what we have identified in the previous section as institutional epistemology. All the key social forces and processes involved (rivalry, exchange, information, and knowledge processes, etc.) are working together due to a very special configuration or concatenation of institutional structures. A discussion regarding the functionality and feasibility of such a complex phenomenon goes above and beyond any formal structure for speculation regarding optimal allocation in equilibrium. It is a truly social theory of the economic calculation phenomena and, by implication, of institutional feasibility.

4.7 A Compounded Theoretical Apparatus

We are now in the position to understand the emerging new Austrian vision and its materialization in a compounded theoretical apparatus that captures the structural and functional links between the exchange dimension and the rivalry dimension within the institutional architecture of a market economy. Economic calculation is predicated on the interface of both. The feasibility of economic arrangements starts at this interface.

Based on the integrated vision described, one can locate the analysis of feasibility in a theoretical model encompassing three interrelated elements: conflict theory (rivalry), institutional theory, and knowledge process theory (prices theory). Together, these three elements create a comprehensive framework that provides a nuanced understanding of the market economy, of the economic calculation, and by implication of the feasibility issue. Conflict theory highlights the importance of competition. Institutional theory emphasizes the role of institutions in channeling this competition productively. And knowledge process theory underscores the significance of prices in facilitating economic coordination.

This theoretical apparatus could be extended to the discussion of all alternative economic systems. In any system, the rivalry situation, the presence of situations expressing forms of zero-sum logics is unavoidable. Same thing regarding various forms of social exchange. The question is this: How is the system going to deal with the rivalry situation? How is it going to connect it to the exchange situation? Is it going to have the appropriate social mechanisms and incentives in the institutional framework, able to generate a structure that will channel them in productive directions via specific forms of social exchange? Is it going to try to suppress them?

The idea of simply eliminating rivalry situations is naïve. Seen in this light, the notion that there will be systems in which zero-sum situations are inexistent is not a realistic basis for debate. The same logic applies to exchange. And assuming, for the sake of argument, the inexistence of rivalry, then we have to contemplate the scenario that will make impossible advanced, complex economic systems. How these systems are to be labeled more specifically, it's in the end a semantic issue and secondary.

In this respect, socialism's problem (as an institutional design) is that it needs to provide a credible institutional structure able to productively convert the rivalrous element in its system. Any system has to regulate conflict and rivalry at least to keep it under control (if not to channel it in more positive directions). Any alternative system, irrespective of the label, needs to deal with that problem. When attempts to suppress rivalry are made, chains of processes incapacitated by the attempts at suppression (or its disconnection from the rest of the system) need to be substituted with a functional equivalent.

Exchange relationships create similar problems in systems that try to suppress them. The implications for the way social conflict, competition, and rivalry are managed in those systems are massive. One of the most interesting aspects revealed by such alternative forms of coordination of production and distribution introduced by socialist systems as substitutes during the grand social experiments of the twentieth century, was that, in the end, rivalry and exchange were not circumvented or eliminated. They were simply displaced and rechanneled in ways that did not harness them toward productive and constructive activity. The internal structure of incentives and information thus created encouraged the emergence of black markets, evasive and unproductive entrepreneurship, and an entire infrastructure of knowledge processes operating with a view to navigating the stringencies of a shortage economy and soft budget constraints. None of that was conductive to dynamic allocative efficiency. In other words, it was not supporting economic growth.

To sum up: The focus on the function and impact of rivalry in social systems open up a broader picture, illuminating how various institutional and exchange arenas contribute to emergent, aggregated processes and outcomes. This perspective shines a light on the significant role specific structures, governance, and economic arrangements play in regulating and structuring rivalry situations, particularly those resembling zero-sum games, which are prevalent in social spaces. When viewed through the lens of institutional theory, these competitive dynamics are not merely left unchecked. Instead, institutions act as mediators, transforming potentially destructive dyadic rivalry into productive systemic competition. This transformation is achieved through regulations, norms, and practices that protect rights, align incentives, solve collective action problems, and channel competitive energies toward constructive ends.

Knowledge process theory, particularly the theory of prices, illuminates how prices are critical in connecting these rivalry situations to exchange arrangements. In this context, prices are not just outcomes of supply and demand interactions but are crucial vehicles for conveying actionable knowledge and information. They aggregate the multifaceted aspects of market interactions, reflecting the complex interplay of rivalry, competition, and cooperation. Prices, therefore, become instrumental in translating what could be zero-sum games into positive, productive systemic results. At the same time, in a very interesting way, they become a regulator of social conflict.

In brief, the neo-Austrian social theory of the market process, as it has evolved in the past forty years by developing its institutionalist and conflict theory pillars, recentres the debate, showing not only how rivalry and competition, guided and structured by institutions and manifested in prices and other market signals, contribute to overall systemic efficiency and productivity, but also how at the same time the price and market signals operate in complex modern societies as regulators of social conflict and as means of social stabilization.

4.8 Conclusions

We are now in a position to reconsider the lessons and the implications of the economic calculation debate for our discussion of the feasibility issue. Obviously, the first thing to be noted is the fact that the feasibility of socialist institutional designs is a subset of problems within the larger class of problems regarding institutional feasibility. Therefore, there is a potential for generalizing about it, but that potential should not be overestimated or misdirected.

That being said, let us follow Schumpeter's way of summing up and framing his own analysis of the economic calculation problem and the controversies associated with it and take his approach as a foil. We'll build on Lavoie's own reading of Schumpeter and expand on it. Schumpeter, explains Lavoie, considers that the debate is built around three separate questions: (a) the theoretical possibility, (b) the practicability in principle, and (c) the relative efficiency of socialism from an economic point of view.

The theoretical possibility question is "whether or not there is anything wrong with the pure logic of a socialist economy." That pure logic is, as we have seen, the static equilibrium formulation of the economic calculation solution. He asks the question whether conditions of behavior and data aggregation in a socialist system will "yield equations that are independent, compatible – that is, free from contradiction – and sufficient in number to determine uniquely the unknowns of the problem before the central board or ministry of production." His response to this query is a resounding affirmation without any reservations, without asking any questions regarding the sources and nature of the data.

Yet as a purely theoretical possibility, one could imagine any logically consistent system or any functionally operational system, given some stringent assumptions about knowledge, incentive, human behavior, and a strict control of emergent propensities and unintended consequences. As long as those assumptions are well calibrated and the rules of deduction are properly applied, one may declare any imagined system to be a theoretical possibility and a matter of equation building and equation solving. This type of exercise may be called "feasibility analysis," or "feasibility condition exploration." However, that is obviously a semantic squabble. In fact, it is an exercise in basic theoretical reasoning, mimicking an exercise in the realm of practical reason.

Is that all what is left to say when it comes to the theoretically possible? Probably not. But that is not what Schumpeter and those following him had in mind. We have seen that there are theoretical approaches in which we are looking at the means-ends models' logic and their application based on an instrumental relationship, in order to determine the feasibility of the systems and their operating structures and mechanisms. In a sense, this is the direction of Schumpeter's second question.

That is what Schumpeter calls the "practicability principle." Schumpeter posits that he can effortlessly refute this argument too, a task he undertakes with a succinct remark implying that a mere review of their resolution to the theoretical challenge will persuade any reader of its practical applicability: "A glance at our solution to the theoretical problem will convince the reader that it is eminently operational." In his view, Schumpeter is confident that the theoretical groundwork he has laid is not only sound but also pragmatically feasible, countering the skepticism posed by Hayek.

However, that is far from evident. It is in this context that the real dimensions of the issue of feasibility, in its most fundamental sense, become most apparent. Our discussions have illuminated the complexity and richness of this field, particularly through our exploration of (a) the NIE approach and its insights and (b) the neo-Austrian social theory of economic calculation. Our case study has demonstrated that addressing this type of question requires the mobilization of theoretical resources and instruments that go way beyond formal analysis and deductions from principles and models. From Lange to Lavoie, we have seen that it is unavoidable to develop some elements of institutional and social theory. This necessitates moving beyond the confines of axiomatics or the logic of choice models, calling for a significant engagement with social sciences theorizing and institutional analysis.

The question then becomes: What is the suitable conceptual and theoretical framework for conducting these investigations? Through our case study, we observed how following step by step the arguments led to the emergence of a social theory framework within three key facets: conflict, exchange, and institutions. This tripartite framework has not only emerged as a significant analytical tool but also offers a robust setting, paving the way for more nuanced and informed analyses of institutional feasibility in various contexts.

Finally, there is Schumpeter's third consideration: the relative efficiency of socialism compared with capitalism. In this respect, his position may be seen as paradoxical. First, he asserts that "pure theory contributes little to the solution of these problems." All that it manages to do is "help us to pose them correctly and to narrow the range of justifiable differences of opinion." But then, in a rather surprising way, he simply states that "we need only glance at the implications of our proof of the possibility and practicability of the socialist schema in order to realize that there is a strong case for believing in its superior economic efficiency."

The evolution of the economic calculation debate has indicated that in approaching the problem of institutional feasibility, we must transcend pure theoretical exercises, incorporating a critical and theoretically informed examination of institutional and social factors. Hence, both the application of the pragmatic logic of means and ends analysis and an analytical framework stepped into the social theory attuned to the risks and uncertainties of social life are needed. By carefully studying what happened in the economic calculation debate as a case study and as an example of feasibility analysis, and by following the NIE and the Neo-Austrian social theory insights, we are in the position to understand the real nature of the challenge and to avoid the trap of reductionism and formalism.

Yet, that being said, a measure of formalism is absolutely necessary in order to discipline our thinking about the feasible and the possible. But the center of gravity and focus of that formalism need to be situated at a rather different level from where it was concentrated during the initial stages of the economic calculation debate. While equilibrium theory has been focal in the discussions of the feasibility issue, the logical and philosophical structures of thinking about the possible and the feasible should take a much more salient role, than speculating about conditions of equilibrium and optimal allocation. The next section will focus on those structures of thinking.

5 The Feasible: Conceptualization and Formalization at the Boundaries of Ideal Theory

This section aims to outline and explore the problem of feasibility and the limits of possibilism from a foundational, formal perspective. It will identify and discuss the formal elements of conceptualizing and thinking about realizability, feasibility, and desirability. As such, it will offer a complementary perspective to the previous sections, pointing out aspects related to the discipline imposed by the logic and "grammar" of thinking and arguing about feasibility and related concepts.

While the previous sections used as vehicles applied level theorizing on the lines of institutional diversity and economic calculation problems, this section approaches the issue from a formal analysis perspective, utilizing its methods as a vehicle as developed in the literature influenced by contemporary logical analysis and analytical philosophy. The objective is to go beyond the space of social economic and governance theorizing and offer the reader a sense of the complexities underlying the discourse and arguments regarding alternative economic and governance systems and the problem of consistently thinking about their feasibility.

With this end in view, the section will start by building a bridge to the previous sections, using the Koopmans–Montias framework as a means to connect the terminology of institutional theory and market process theory with the frameworks and formal theories discussed in this section. Once the junction point is provided, the section will proceed as follows: With the concepts of desirability, realizability, and feasibility introduced and connections between these concepts established, the discussion will first focus on the possibilist analysis in assessing economic systems. The section will continue with (i) a discussion of feasibility and realizability, in which feasibility is seen as a variety of realizability, followed by (ii) the semantical approach to feasibility, including an exploration of the properties of accessibility relations (reflexivity, seriality, transitivity, and finiteness) and their implications for the concept of feasibility and how we use it, and (iii) an outline of the syntactical analysis of feasibility and how the "grammar of feasibility" shapes our understanding of feasibility. The last part of the section engages with the issue of desirability and ideal theory, projecting the formal approach presented in the first part on the background of the broader and more intuitively clear themes of the tension between ideal and nonideal theory and the role of ideal theory in guiding transitions from nonideal to ideal states.

5.1 Desirable, Realizable, and Feasible and the Koopmans–Montias Framework

The three concepts: desirable, realizable, and feasible are closely connected. They all apply to the same objects. It is natural to identify these objects with actual or possible states of affairs. However, some qualifications must be introduced. First, it is necessary to indicate the context in which they are to be identified. For example, consider again the Comparative Economic Systems Koopmans–Montias framework introduced in Section 3. In this framework, an economy is describable a structure $\varepsilon = (e, s, p_s, o)$, where an outcome $o = f(e, s, p_s)$. Second, both quantitative and qualitative outcomes can be evaluated by applying criteria n (called norms). Third, at each point of evaluation an economy ε is in a global state σ_ε of affairs, given by certain values of the indices defining ε: the environment (e), the economic system (s) and the government policies conducted within the system (p_s). Realizable, feasible, or desirable states of affairs are included in such global states σ_ε an economy ε might be in.

This option has important consequences. It moves us to the conceptual area of possibilist analysis. In this framework, an economy ε is given as a complex class Σ_ε of possible states σ_ε. The focus of analysis consists of two aspects: First, we need to provide some criteria to determine the class of such admissible states of affairs, that is, states that can be taken as objects of analysis. Given the structure $\varepsilon = (e, s, p_s, o)$, some values of its components are of course excluded, that is, some possible states σ are not accepted. Clearly, we cannot accept a configuration of such values that is logically inconsistent; a state σ of ε may also be not admissible for different other reasons: It may be physically impossible, or morally unacceptable, and so on. We shall argue that such constraints on the size and scope of the class of admissible states of ε are crucial for understanding the three concepts.

The second aspect concerns the fact that the cross-connections among different admissible states of ε become essential. On the one hand, they show which transitions from a state of affairs σ_ε to another state σ'_ε are possible or acceptable on certain criteria, and which are not. Formally, these cross-connections can be regarded as relations on the class Σ_ε of admissible states. These relations can be of different types. The most common are binary, but we shall also argue that ternary relations are sometimes appealed to in the attempts to account for the idea of desirability. Let σ_ε be a state of the economy ε. It may move from σ_ε to some states, but not to others: in other words, some states are accessible for ε from σ_ε, while others are not; a transition of ε from σ_ε to them is or is not admissible. So we can define a binary relation on the class Σ_ε. The appeal to such relations helps us give the meaning of claims like: The state that σ_ε is realizable or is feasible, or desirable. Two observations are immediate: first, given that what is accessible from one state of affairs might not be so from another, realizability, feasibility, and desirability can only be defined relative to a certain context (economy ε) and only relative to a given state σ_ε of it. Second, to define these properties comes to showing how the accessibility relations R are constructed. In what follows we shall assume that an economy ε is fixed.

We shall start with the concept of realizability. Then we shall discuss feasibility as a variety of realizability. Finally, we shall show what desirability brings new for understanding feasibility.

5.2 Approaching Feasibility

In a basic sense, to say that a state of affairs σ' is realizable from σ means that a transition from σ to σ' is possible. This assumes that σ' is not logically inconsistent and also complies with the "laws of nature." This second constraint needs some clarifications. Our current theories of natural sciences (physics, chemistry, and biology) point to state of affairs that are possible and state of affairs that are not possible. Analogously, some states of affairs are compatible with the fundamental mechanisms of human psychology and human capacities, and also with general facts about human societies. Such constraints express exactly what we take as possible in an absolute sense: Some state of affairs cannot be included in the set of states Σ_ε an economy ε might be in because of metaphysical, logical, scientific, or even technological reasons. For example, even if much desired, we cannot construct a *perpetuum mobile*. A relative sense of the possible is involved when we note that given a state of affairs σ some other state is not accessible, because of, for example, economic, institutional, and cultural conditions: a state of affairs of a given economy, at a given moment makes some outcomes impossible; but they are possible for another economy or even for that economy at another moment, or under different circumstances.

Taking realizability to express the notions of absolute or pure relative possibility helps us provide a more specific and detailed definition of feasibility. Three accounts of it have been proposed (Southwood 2018). The first is a cost-based account: according to it, feasibility is to be understood in terms of what is achievable without undue costs. Non-feasibility occurs whenever, although a transition to a targeted state of affairs is possible in terms of logical, nomological, political, and technological aspects, the costs of it are socially perceived as imposing an unbearable cost. To turn Switzerland's economy into a communist centralized one is possible, but the costs of the transition are incomprehensively high. According to a second, probability-based account, a state σ is feasible for an agent or a set (or even a group) of agents if there are good reasons to accept that σ would be if the agent(s) were to try to realize it. As Estlund (2014) argues, this view must be understood not as involving the ability of the agent to realize σ, but an objective probability: σ is feasible when there is good chance that they will do it, that the (objective) probability of their doing it is not close to zero.

Institutional Diversity and Economic Calculation

A third, possibility-based account is perhaps the most attractive. It persuades us to understand feasibility as a specific kind of possibility or realizability. Logicians study possibility (and necessity) in two main ways: syntactically and semantically. Syntactically, they study the grammar of expressions like "it is possible that" and "it is necessary that" and try to identify the properties of the more complex expressions of the language in which they occur. The standard semantical approach to possibility appeals to the so-called possible worlds framework. A possible world is a way the world might be: It consists in a maximally consistent set of states of affairs. In our case, a world is a global state of affairs σ_ε an economy ε might be in. The worlds contain specific, "local" states of affairs; they are referred to when we describe, in our case for example, certain characteristics of the environment e, or of the system s, or the policy enforced in the economy in a state σ. These states of affairs are expressed as sentences and we shall denote them by letters φ, ψ, and so on. The basic intuition in using the framework is rooted in the philosophy of Leibniz. For him φ's being necessary is its being realized in all possible worlds, and φ's being possible is its being realized in some possible world. We shall base our research on the possible worlds semantics. But since the worlds we investigate are states σ of an economy, we shall substitute talk about worlds with talk about such states σ of an economy.

Global states of an economy (or, say, of a society) are very large and very complex entities. Taking them as basic units of analysis opens the possibility to take into account a huge variety of variables. But it also allows the possibility to address more specific aspects. When trying to see if some state φ of affairs is feasible, we need not assume that all the aspects and processes in an economy have to be taken into account, and can focus only on some relevant parts of it. Of course, what is of relevance depends upon the preferences of the actors involved, and upon the resources they have in a given context. Therefore, what is feasible is discerned in some narrower contexts. For example, Ostrom (2005, 14) argued that to study action arenas one needs to extract from the complexity of the reality only a small number of variables. However, the appeal to global states offers the formal theoretical background for such analyses.

We note from the very beginning that all three accounts of feasibility have a basic presupposition: They treat it in relation to, or even as determined by what the actor(s) involved act or intend to do. This entails that the notion of feasibility cannot be simply understood as absolute or relative realizability. Moreover, it is distinct from conceivability: feasibility assumes actors' agency, and their capacity to make changes in the world. Obviously, to say that a state of affairs is feasible today is not to say that it is conceivable. A person may conceive a world in which in the next two decades a hundred of millions of humans colonized

Jupiter's satellite Io, but we would hardly agree that this is feasible. Feasibility must take into account our resources and dispositions to act in a certain way. Wiens (2015a) argued that all our technological, institutional, motivational (and so on) means we have on hand (what he calls "our current total stock of all-purpose resources") must be addressed to get a useful notion of feasibility.

As a consequence, the proponents of the possibility-based account typically treat feasibility as instantiating a more restricted notion of realizability. To give it a more precise treatment, it is natural to appeal to the apparatus of modal logic. This is what Wiens (2015a) tries to do. In terms of the semantics of the possible worlds, a specific state of affairs φ of an economy ε is feasible relative to a reference global state of affairs σ, if, for a well-specified sense of "accessible," it is contained in some world (state of affairs σ') accessible from it; and it is not feasible if there is no such accessible world. To be more rigorous, write $R(\sigma, \sigma')$ to express the fact that the global state of affairs σ' is accessible from σ. Then a state of affairs φ is feasible at some global state σ if relation $R(\sigma, \sigma')$ holds and φ is realized at σ', that is, starting from the state σ there is an R-transition to σ' in which φ holds.

Relying on the possible worlds frame has important consequences. First, it focuses the attention on the role of contextual and circumstantial configurations of variables under study. This is given by the various possible states of an economy and the specific transitions among them. Thus, feasibility is conceptualized quite specifically, by taking into account context. Second, transitions among states are not strictly determined in one way or another: as we shall immediately show, the R-type relations detected may satisfy quite different properties. Finally, the possible worlds frame does not require an appeal to general laws. The role of laws is rendered by the set of admissible possible worlds (global states of an economy) and the cross-connections between them (R-type relations and the transitions they admit).

In the next section, we shall explore in more detail the option of understanding feasibility in terms of restricted possibility, in both a syntactical and a semantical perspective. We shall define more rigorously what such restrictions consist in and we shall explore the relevance of the different configurations of possible "worlds." At the same time, from a syntactical perspective, we shall investigate the grammar of feasibility: How these restrictions configure the ways we use the term. For the syntax and semantics of modal logic see for example Bull and Segerberg (2001). This approach to feasibility helps uncover the structural properties of our use of the concept. (Unfortunately, these structural properties of the accessibility relation were ignored in the recent growing literature on feasibility A notable exception is Wiens 2015b).

5.3 The Semantical Approach

The semantical approach to feasibility centers on the properties the accessibility relation R between two global states of affairs σ and σ' may have. We shall test a few such properties and discuss how they fit our ordinary understanding of feasibility. Note from the very beginning that the fact that R-type relations are not conceived as complete, that is, as connecting any two states of an economy, but subject to some more specific properties and limitations is an expression of the intuition that change is to be viewed in relation to human agency and human creativity. The step-by-step definition of R makes sense of the fact (forcefully put by Hirschman's possibilism) that individuals and groups use complex resources and develop new institutional arrangements to overcome the obstacles they meet.

(i) A somehow trivial property of R is its reflexivity: any state of affairs σ is accessible from itself. This is intended to say that once a state of affairs is realized in a state σ, it must be assumed as feasible.

(ii) Another property relation R may have is seriality: no situation is a dead end – for each σ the actors have the capacity to act so that to achieve a new situation. Consider again the case of a socialist economy. As Ward (1967) emphasized, it faces the problem of allocating resources such that it will be able to function with a tolerable degree of efficiency. This means that for each state σ of it there must be some feasible alternative to it. For otherwise it would collapse.

(iii) A more informative property of R is transitivity. Let both $R(\sigma, \sigma')$ and $R(\sigma', \sigma'')$ hold: The state of affairs σ' is accessible from σ and σ'' is accessible form σ'. Transitivity requires that $R(\sigma, \sigma'')$, that is, σ'' must also be accessible from σ. Now suppose that some state of affairs φ is not the case at σ, and even more, it is not feasible at σ: in spite of all the efforts of the actors, they cannot turn φ into an actual state of affairs at any accessible state σ'. However, there is a state σ'' which is accessible from some such state σ' and φ holds at it: so, it is feasible to achieve at σ'. By transitivity, φ must also be regarded as feasible at σ. Transitivity requires that feasibility should be understood in this broader sense, to include both what we can achieve directly and indirectly.

Similarly, Rawls (1999, 12) argues that "there are questions about how the limits of the practicably possible are discerned and what the conditions of our social world in fact are. The problem here is that the limits of the possible are not given by the actual, for we can to a greater or lesser extent change political and social institutions and much else." The practicably possible Rawls has in mind is another name of the feasible. When he asserts that its limits are not given by what is actual, he means that although some state of affairs φ is not actually feasible, it might be so, under some modified conditions. Those modified conditions point, however, to a different situation, which is actually feasible. So, his assertion is that although some φ is not feasible, it is still possible that φ is feasible at some accessible situations.

The same idea is supported by Gilabert and Lawford-Smith (2012). For them, both what we can achieve directly, that is, from here and now, and indirectly, that is, by putting ourselves in a position to achieve them, are within the scope of the feasible. To include what we can achieve indirectly in the scope of the feasible is to accept transitivity.

Transitivity is presupposed if we take into consideration cases in which achieving a situation requires a change of the institutional arrangements. Even if a state of affairs is not accessible given certain institutional economic and political arrangements, appropriate changes may make it accessible and thus feasible.

"Path-dependence" approaches are also committed to transitivity. They take the future options to be strongly determined by present choices (actions and policies), to the extent that some of them can result in irrevocably closing off certain future accessible situations. Following the routes open at σ narrow the options. As we move guided by R, no new accessible global state of the economy is attained.

However, one can argue that moving from one world to another may well result not only in closing some possibilities but also in opening new ones. A state of affairs that is unfeasible at σ may turn into a feasible one at some global state σ' accessible from σ. Incrementalists position on this side. For them not only means, but also ends may change in some transitions. As we move from one situation to another, it is possible to have $R(\sigma, \sigma')$ and $R(\sigma', \sigma'')$, but not $R(\sigma, \sigma'')$. Similarly, if an ideal society is viewed as an institutional arrangement fundamentally or even radically distinct from the actual situation σ_0, it is regarded as a long-term target (Wiens 2015a). But, since it is only a long-term target, the ideal is not actually feasible, although it might be feasibly feasible (i.e. actually feasible at some accessible step). Moreover, in cases in which a type of ideal theory is not appealed to in order to guide social choice, it is possible that some transitions to certain states of affairs be ignored, although they are reachable by appropriate institutional changes, and this makes transitivity collapse.

(iv) Another property the accessibility relation R may satisfy is finiteness: It looks natural to say that a state φ is feasible only if it can be achieved in a finite number of steps, preferably in a foreseeable future. This means that there is a finite number of states such that $R(\sigma, \sigma_1)$ and $R(\sigma_1, \sigma_2)$ ... and $R(\sigma_{n-1}, \sigma_n)$ and φ is realized in σ_n. If transitivity is also assumed, this means that φ is feasible from σ. To require that a state of affairs is achievable in a reasonable time, through a reasonable number of steps is a natural condition.

An argument for accepting this property of the accessibility relation is that in each possible situation, our means for altering the status quo are finite: resources (including money and technology) are limited, the ways in which they can be used are not unbounded, actors have limited capacity and motivation to follow a usually distant aim, existing institutions are not able to convers any type of resources to a desired target, not all allocation of resources is possible, and so on (Wiens 2015a). Therefore, the feasible must be reached in a finite number of steps.

5.4 The Grammar of Feasibility

From a syntactical point of view, the question is how the expression "it is feasible that φ" is used; in other words, we need to uncover its grammar. For simplicity, in what follows we shall write $F\varphi$ for it. The possible worlds apparatus proved to be attractive because it showed that there are systematic relations between the properties we attribute to the accessibility relation R and the grammar of the feasible: to use $F\varphi$ in a certain way is to assume that the relation R has some property. We shall show that this is the case by focusing on the four properties of R we mentioned earlier:

Suppose that R is reflexive. Then everything that is realized at a situation σ is also realized in an achievable situation (σ itself). So, we have: if φ is realized, then it is feasible, or more formally: if φ, then $F\varphi$. Prima facie, it is not intuitively true. For even if φ happens to hold at σ, it does not follow that it is realized because some agent(s) brought it about. Its being actual at σ might depend on quite other reasons. However, there are some contexts counting in its favor. Think about a system of governance of a common resourcethat proved to be robust, that is, it has a long-term success (Ostrom 2005; Ostrom 2014). In terms of accessibility, once implemented, the institutional arrangements characterizing the system are resilient given different transitions. More formally, this means that what is realized at some state must also be regarded as feasible: The accessibility relation is reflexive.

Second, suppose that R is serial. Then for each situation σ there is some situation σ' which is achievable from σ. This means that for any state of affairs φ either it is realized at σ' or $\sim\varphi$ is realized at σ'. Which means that either φ is feasible at σ, or $\sim\varphi$ is feasible at σ: $F\varphi$ or $F\sim\varphi$.

Third, consider transitivity of R. We show that it is given by the following expression: if it is feasible that φ is feasible, then indeed φ is feasible (or: if $FF\varphi$, then $F\varphi$). For let σ be a state of an economy ε. The expression mentioned previously states that, if some state of affairs φ is feasible under some modified conditions, then it must also be actually feasible. That is, suppose that at some state σ' reachable from σ the state of affairs φ is feasible and so it is the case at some state σ'' reachable from σ'. If R is transitive, then σ'' is reachable from σ and thus, because φ is the case at σ'', it follows that φ is feasible at σ.

We finally move to the constraint that a state φ is feasible if it can be reached in a finite number of steps. For a formal treatment of this condition see van Benthem (2001, 349). One way in which it is expressed in the grammar of the feasible is this: We accept that if $F\varphi$, then it is also feasible that φ is realized while it is not feasible that φ. Thus, if some state of affairs is feasible and it comes to be realized in some situation, there can be no other transition to another situation in which it would still; if attained, that situation cannot be surpassed. In other words, if reachable at all, this happens in a finite sequence of steps.

Our analysis allows us to present the abstract formula which captures the basic components of the concept of feasibility and summarizes the grammar of feasibility:

It is feasible for X to α in the context Z to bring about a state of affairs σ in which φ is realized.

In line with our approach in the previous sections, in this definition of feasibility, the concept of context is pivotal. We argued that the context Z must be specified in a complex sense: claims about feasibility are always done relative to a specific economy (or society) $\varepsilon = (e, s, p_s, o)$ and also to a given global state of affairs of it. A state of affairs φ is included in a global state σ and represents the possible result of the action α of the agent(s) X. We have already mentioned that feasibility presupposes a reference to an actor or a set of actors X and thus it presupposes their agency: What is feasible expresses not only what may happen to happen, but what can be regarded as an effect of human agency.

However, the analysis of these components of the formula confronts hard difficulties. They stem from the fact that actors may be individual or collective. When the context consists in an economy ε, actors are groups or collectives, rather than individuals: corporations, trade unions, non-governmental organizations, but also political parties, governmental agencies and more complex coalitions of such actors. Two types of such collective actions must be distinguished. First, the decision a group is to come to may be the result of an aggregative procedure. In this case, the apparatus developed by public choice and social choice theorists is essential for providing an adequate treatment of collective-choice. Second, some actions of a group cannot be accounted for in this aggregative sense. They are joint actions: an orchestra's playing a symphony or a football team's constructing a defense strategy are not reducible to the individual actions of the members of the group. J. Searle (1995, 2010), Tuomela (2013), and Gilbert (2014) are main proponents of this approach.

It is plausible to argue that some of these groups constitute group agents (Pettit and List 2012) and can be regarded as capable of agency. But in many other cases, this is not the case. Moreover, even if a group arguably constitutes a collective agent, the attempts to make sense of "collective agency", "collective intentions" as irreducible to the actions and the intentions of the individual members of the group did not succeed to convince. As Vincent Ostrom (1997, 106) writes, "collectivities may act in concert and function as actors, but group actions are always to be understood as patterned forms of individual actions." Therefore, the primitive idea is that of an individual action, while group concepts can be analyzed in institutional terms, that is, in terms of induced patterns of individual actions.

The formula includes a crucial reference to the action α performed by the actor(s) X. While in practice there is no clear distinction between an act and its effect, it is useful to analytically distinguish between α and the state of affairs φ. One reason is that, by α-ing, the actor(s) actually bring about a larger state of affairs in which φ is contained. We can identify it with a global state σ. Now σ may include many other components than strictly φ, such as non-intended but foreseen effects of doing α, as well as non-intended and even non-foreseen effect of α-ing; moreover, when α-ing the actor X may have assumed some intended results which did not realize.

A deeper issue is this: it is usually assumed that the account of feasibility must make sense of a fundamental characteristic of human agency: it is always directed to a target. Note also an ambiguity concerning the agency of X: by α-ing, the actor(s) may bring about one of the different global states of affairs σ_1, σ_2 . . ., with the property that φ is realized in each of them. But feasibility only requires that φ be realized. This observation has important consequences. Consider the following example: an increase in the welfare of all the members of the society is feasible; but this can be done by implementing different social policies, and some of them may be inacceptable, because they are incompatible with other objectives of the government. This shows that the target state of affairs intended by α-ing must be the particular φ, not the global state σ in which φ is contained. Consequently, we shall modify the abstract formula presented earlier as follows:

> It is feasible for X to α in the context Z to bring about a state of affairs σ in which the target φ is realized.

This formula shows that the accessibility relation R between a global state of affairs σ and another global state σ' can be defined by taking into account these components of an action situation. For different actors and their actions, in different contexts and for different targets, the accessibility relation is usually different. For example, different groups in the society prefer different policies p_s and therefore some transitions may be acceptable for some R but not for other relations. In all these cases, the job of the accessibility relation R is to show how the possible transitions between two global states of affairs are restricted: even if logically or metaphysically possible, a given relation R may prohibit some transitions, while other relations R' would allow them.

5.5 Desirability and the Ideal Theory

The case is even more difficult to manage when the outcomes in the achieved state σ' are to be evaluated (in terms of some norm) with respect to the success in realizing the target φ. The appeal to a norm, in the sense of Koopmans–Montias to make feasibility assessments can be pursued by addressing technical standards, like efficiency, productivity, and so on. The target expressed by φ may simply consist in what the actor(s) X desire to do, in their capacity of free persons. But usually, targets have a normative or moral component: They are conceived as incorporating the values or the ideals actors have. Realizing φ in σ is an objective not only desired, but desirable: a state of affairs σ' in which φ holds is worth realizing from a moral standpoint. Such targets are constructed with respect to a variety of moral, political, ecological or religious values and ideals.

Viewing targets as normatively laden may entail two types of inconsistencies, external and internal. Internal inconsistencies concern the impossibility to realize simultaneously two or more ideals. Ideally, we would like to have both maximal liberty and perfect equality among the members of the society. But perhaps achieving more equality requires the implementation of policies consisting in restrictions on the liberty of free exchanges. In general, if more ideal targets are assumed, no feasible transition would succeed in achieving a state of affairs in which they all are fully realized.

A natural reaction in such cases is to consider that, although a state in which all ideal conditions are realized is beyond feasibility, the desirable target is one in which most of those conditions are realized. The target to be achieved is one that best resembles the ideal state. However, this line of argument is misleading. As Lipsey and Lancaster (1956, 12) put it, "it is *not* true that a situation in which more, but not all, of the optimum conditions are fulfilled is necessarily, or is even likely to be, superior to a situation in which fewer are fulfilled." According to their theory of the second best, we need to refrain from assuming naively that implementing more of the components of the ideal state, or implementing them to a greater degree is better than implementing less, or implementing them to a lesser degree. "Where one or more of our wishes cannot be completely met (which is, after all, the only world in which trade-offs are required at all), arrangements that are slightly less than ideal in all dimensions might be better than arrangements that are absolutely ideal in all but one" (Goodin 1995, 54). For example, although liberty is an ideal, in conditions of economic underdevelopment, perhaps less of liberty might actually be better than more. This shows that feasibility and desirability are deeply entangled and that the preference for one of them must always be contextually determined.

External inconsistencies arise when there is a conflict between what is realistically achievable and what is normatively desirable. This tension reflects an old philosophical principle: *ought implies can*. In some cases, pursuing a feasible course of action may undermine our ability to realize moral ideals. Conversely, striving to fulfill normative goals – such as greater equity – may render efficient or practical solutions unattainable. When feasibility takes precedence, moral aspirations often become harder to achieve. Attention to facts and constraints gains importance, while normative demands may be sidelined. On the other hand, when normative desirability is prioritized, the goal is to uphold moral principles – even if this means disregarding certain empirical realities. As a result, political theory tends to split in two directions: one that emphasizes feasibility and shows strong sensitivity to social facts, and another that upholds normative ideals, sometimes at the expense of engaging with those facts.

This tension between the perfect realization of an ideal in a postulated state of affairs and the quite imperfect real-world instantiation of the ideal is the subject-matter of the largely debated issue of the ideal versus nonideal theory. It involves two moves. From nonideal to ideal theory, the move concerns the feasible transitions required to reach the ideal desirable target, starting with the actual nonideal state of affairs of the society. In this case, transitions are assumed to obey not only effectiveness restrictions but also normative (moral and political) ones.

The second move is from ideal to nonideal theory. Human collective action is to a large extent guided by posited ideals; however, usually, we find a deep gap between the moral and political principles appropriate to defining the ideal conditions in the target state of affairs and the real-world circumstances. Therefore, the analysis of these transitions concerns "the way in which we may use normative principles derived at the level of ideal theory to guide our attempts at assessing and improving our current state of the world, which is bound to be characterized by different circumstances than the ones we stipulated in order to generate our normative principles" (Volacu 2017).

The ideal theory is assumed to guide members of the society in their relations and in their designing common institutions for their mutual benefit: "nonideal theory presupposes that ideal theory is already on hand. For until the ideal is identified, at least in outline – and that is all we should expect – nonideal theory lacks an objective, an aim, by reference to which its queries can be answered" (Rawls 1999, 89–90). Such a guidance is two-dimensional. A first dimension is substantial: It posits an objective, an aim which is identified as an ideal state of affairs of the society, which eventually would be achieved. A second dimension is procedural: The ideal theory is prioritized in the sense that it offers guidance for real-world nonideal cases. It helps design policies and construct institutions that would make feasible the transition from the actual state of affairs to another state closer to the assumed objective, but it does not require the reification of some ideal state of affairs. The two dimensions are distinct and, as we shall argue, they entail distinct accounts of the relations between feasibility and (normative) desirability.

On the substantial dimension, two main questions need to be answered: What is the status of the ideal state, and how is it related to real-world circumstances? The approach offered by J. Rawls is usually the starting point for discussing these questions. For Rawls, the ideal state – what he calls the "original position" – models two things: First, the morally appropriate conditions in which the terms of cooperation are to be established; and second the acceptable restrictions on the basis of which the principles of justice are to be selected. Thus, its role is that of a "device of representation or, alternatively, a thought-experiment for the purpose of public- and self-clarification" (Rawls 2001, 17).

The original position is a theoretical construct obtained by a process of idealization. Idealization is an essential part of scientific practice, implicated in theory building, designing experiments and explanation. It signifies "a deliberate simplifying of something complicated (a situation, a concept, etc.) with a view to achieving at least at a partial understanding of that thing. It may involve a distortion of the original or it can simply mean a leaving aside of some components in a complex in order to focus the better on the remaining ones" (McMullin 1985, 248).

So, a first type of idealization occurs when intentionally one distorts a component of the real-world situation. For example, when physicists study the movement of a ball on a floor, they assume that friction comes closer and closer to zero; the law governing the movement of the ball on the floor is defined in the limit, ideal, case when friction is zero. A similar case is when economists consider situations in which competition becomes more and more perfect, or when political theorists assume that nearly all voters are fully rational. This type of idealization – we call it linear one – lets us control the feasibility of the transitions to new state of affairs, closer and closer to the ideal target, although the ideal state is not reachable.

A second type of idealization is structural: It requires that some components of the real-world situation are eliminated, or replaced by a different one. An instance of it is met in political philosophy. We already noted that the original position is an idealization construct. Rawls models the ideal just society by the notion of original position. An essential feature of it is that its inhabitants "assume that the principles they acknowledge, whatever they are, will be strictly complied with and followed by everyone. Thus, the principles of justice that result are those defining a perfectly just society, given favorable conditions" (Rawls 1971, 245). But strict compliance, which entails that law-breaking is excluded, cannot be obtained in a real-world society. At most, we can imagine just institutional arrangements closer and closer in their characteristics to the perfectly just society. The reason why strict compliance is possible in the ideal society is that its inhabitants are modeled by Rawls in a quite distinctive way. The members of any real (liberal) society are regarded as endowed with two moral powers: They are both reasonable and rational. Being rational means that they have the capacities to form, revise and pursue a conception of the good; and being reasonable means that they have a moral capacity for a sense of justice (to cooperate with others on terms that are fair and to act upon principles of justice and their requirements). They can be more or less rational or reasonable. In the limit, we can imagine a society whose members are most reasonable; but, of course, even there we cannot exclude the possibility that some individuals would break the law. Rawls argues that things are quite different in the ideal society. Its members are represented as rational actors. However, being reasonable is not a property meaningfully attached to them: They are neither reasonable nor unreasonable. Reasonableness is modeled not as a property of individuals, but as built in the structure of the original position: given the veil of ignorance, actors comply with the principles of justice because they are specifically positioned, not in virtue of having a capacity to do this.

As a structural ideal state of affairs, the original position is therefore different in nature from any state of a real society. Therefore, one cannot hope to achieve it; at most it is possible to have a transition to a state close to it. This idea is expressed by Rawls who says that, while the original position is a utopia, it is a "realistic" one: "Political philosophy is realistically Utopian when it extends what are ordinarily thought to be the limits of practicable political possibility and, in so doing, reconciles us to our political and social condition" (Rawls

1999, 11). While Rawls offers some preliminary insights into this process, the complexities involved in bridging the gap between utopian ideals and practical implementation are still not fully resolved, leaving open questions about how these theoretical constructs can be effectively applied in the real world.

Another example of structural idealization is O. Lange's concept of an ideal socialist economy we discussed in the previous section. Referring to Hayek and Robbins, Lange writes: "They do not deny the theoretical possibility of a rational allocation of resources in a socialist economy, they only doubt the possibility of a satisfactory practical solution of the problem" (Lange 1936, 56). In other words, one can imagine an ideal socialist state of an economy, but nonideal theory meets an unsolvable problem on how that state could be reached. Lange also agrees that the idealization required has a specific character: It differs from what happens in a capitalist economy, where the function of the market is to provide a method of allocating resources by trial and error. But a socialist economy is deprived of this characteristic. So, the concept of an ideal socialist economy is based on a structural idealization. Lange's paper tries to show that socialism, in both the special case when freedom of choice in consumption is still allowed, and also when this assumption is nonexistent (i.e., the allocation of resources is directed by the aims and valuations of the socialist bureaucracy) can be made practically possible: so, he concludes, the economic consistency and workability of a socialist economy is demonstrated (1936, 70). However, he admits that the transition to a socialist economy (even far from an ideal one) meets hard, even insuperable problems, and that the process is very difficult to pass through (Lange 1937, 133).

We noted earlier that the ideal theory is assumed to have a guidance role for the members of the society, and that such guidance can be exercised in a substantive or in a procedural sense. In a substantive sense, the ideal theory posits by idealization an ideal state of affairs of an economy or of a society. On a procedural one, the role of the ideal theory is different: It does not reify the target ideal state but constructs mechanisms to assure a transition toward it. Anderson (2010, 3) clearly figures this implication:

> We recognize the existence of a problem before we have any idea of what would be best or most just. Nor do we need to know what is ideal in order to improve. Knowledge of the better does not require knowledge of the best. Figuring out how to address a just claim on our conduct now does not require knowing what system of principles of conduct would settle all possible claims on our conduct in all possible worlds, or in the best of all possible worlds.

Therefore, the notion of an ideal target loses its substantive meaning. It does not need to be conceived as an ideal situation. Rather it gets a different role to play: It would consist in a set of constraints on the grammar of using the terms "possible" and, specifically, "feasible." On this account, moral targets are tools to design routes to situations characterized by better outcomes. The idea that reference to ideal principles of justice must be understood in the sense that they produce the concept of an ideal state is replaced by the claim that they are mechanisms to guide a normatively acceptable and also feasible route to a better state.

James Buchanan (2004, 61) expressed clearly this view on the role of nonideal theory: It guides the approach to ultimate targets by setting intermediate moral targets and also by helping us to determine the means and processes that are feasible, but also morally permissible. This methodological view on the role of social sciences was forcefully promoted by Hayek. For him, "the theories of the social sciences do not consist of "laws" in the sense of empirical rules about the behaviour of objects definable in physical terms. All that the theory of the social sciences attempts is to provide a technique of reasoning which assists us in connecting individual facts, but which, like logic or mathematics, is not about the facts" (Hayek 2014, 90).

The relevance of an approach that assigns a guiding role to theory lies in its ability to navigate the complex terrain of moral and practical decision-making. Instead of fixating on an unattainable ideal state, this approach uses theory to set intermediate moral targets that are both achievable and ethically sound. By doing so, it allows us to determine the means and processes that are not only feasible but also morally permissible, ensuring that our actions align with ethical principles while remaining grounded in real-world possibilities. This approach shifts the focus from striving for an abstract ideal to constructing practical mechanisms that guide us toward better outcomes. It emphasizes that progress does not require a perfect understanding of an ideal state but rather a clear vision of the steps needed to improve our current situation. This pragmatic use of theory, as articulated by thinkers like Hayek and Buchanan, provides a more realistic and actionable framework for addressing the challenges of governance and social justice.

In conclusion, the elements introduced in this section serve as essential instruments for guiding our understanding and analysis of feasibility within the broader context of institutional alternatives. By exploring the concepts of desirability, realizability, and feasibility, we have provided a formal framework that allows us to navigate the complex terrain of economic and governance systems. These conceptual tools help us recognize the constraints and possibilities inherent in different institutional arrangements, offering a structured approach to evaluating what is achievable within given social, economic, and political contexts. This analytical framework is crucial for both theoretical discourse and practical decision-making, ensuring that our assessments of feasibility are grounded in a rigorous understanding of the underlying principles.

Furthermore, the logic behind these debates, as explored through the semantical and syntactical approaches to feasibility, underscores the importance of a nuanced and context-sensitive evaluation of institutional alternatives. The properties of accessibility relations, such as reflexivity, seriality, transitivity, and finiteness, are not merely abstract concepts but practical tools that inform how we think about the potential transitions between different states of affairs. By employing these instruments, we can better anticipate the challenges and opportunities presented by various governance models and institutional designs. Ultimately, this section equips us with the necessary analytical tools to engage more effectively in the ongoing debates about the feasibility of alternative economic and governance systems in the twenty-first century.

6 Conclusions

The study has amply illustrated why the problem of institutional feasibility eludes the efforts to reduce it to a merely formal, speculative exercise of a priori theorizing and abstract modeling or to convert it into a technical approach aiming at the implementation of specific, predefined institutional formulas in applied-level settings. Dealing with the challenge of feasibility requires complex explorations using theoretical, methodological, philosophical, and logical tools able to differentiate the fuzzy and ever-changing border between what may be achievable and what may not be achievable within the constraints of specific historical, economic, and social contexts. The complexity of the issue has thus illuminated the critical role of theoretical, disciplinary, and methodological pluralism in exploring the preconditions and facets of institutional feasibility. Again and again, our investigation has shown why and how dealing with the feasibility issue is a crux of theoretical, empirical, and applied research. Tools from economics, philosophy, and political science converge to address feasibility as a multidimensional problem.

For instance, we have understood how the logical and philosophical inquiry at the boundaries between ideal and nonideal theory, as seen, for instance, in the discussions on accessibility relations and the semantics of feasibility, provides a formal yet flexible framework for addressing in a consistent and logically disciplined manner the transitions between states of affairs in the realm of the possible. Likewise, methodological approaches such as the Koopmans–Montias CES framework or the Ostroms' IAD framework have illustrated the importance of developing tools able to help us conceptualize and analyze context-specific variables and adaptive governance mechanisms. Even more interesting, we have seen how – on the theoretical side – the evolution of the Austrian School's theorizing in response to the avatars of the economic calculation debate over the years has led to the emergence of a compounded theoretical framework grounded in social theory, which captures the multifaceted complexity of institutional feasibility: the structure and functioning of institutional arrangements, the dynamics of rivalry and competition, and the processes of information and knowledge creation.

The economic calculation debate has thus offered an excellent illustration of how the problem of feasibility evolves over time in connection with the development, across generations, of the conceptual and theoretical frameworks that structure and fuel the discourse addressing it. As these frameworks have advanced, they have shaped not only the parameters of the debate but also the methodologies used, moving from static, abstract models to dynamic, empirically grounded, and context-sensitive analyses. In this respect, we have noted that the evolution taking place on the Austrian theory front dovetails with the evolutions on the institutional theory front. In a sense, one may consider that both are converging into a novel institutional epistemology approach to the feasibility issue, even if one may also say that from the very beginning the Austrian take on the problems of economic calculation, the functions of the price systems in a free market economy, and the role of knowledge in society was the epitome of the institutionalist epistemology paradigm.

In any case, the developments on both fronts have put us in the position to reframe the feasibility issue in a fresher light. This reframing integrates the search for feasibility into a larger picture, a picture that captures the ongoing operations of institutions as they enable (or hamper) the continuous adaptation and self-correction in response to real-world challenges. Instead of treating feasibility as an external aspect, this approach embeds its definition, assessment, and implementation within institutional processes themselves, emphasizing the procedures of experimentation, learning, and incremental adjustments. In this view, polycentric systems serve as a critical framework for this approach, with their overlapping decision centers that enable diverse strategies to be tested, refined, and scaled.

The study has repeatedly illuminated that feasibility demands a reconciliation of normative and practical considerations, demonstrating that it is not a purely technical issue of achieving predefined goals given a set of means. For example, the integration of ideal and nonideal theory showcases how normative principles guide the articulation of aspirational goals, while pragmatic, stepwise approaches ensure the feasibility of their attainment. In the emerging institutional epistemology, the interplay between desirability and feasibility, is a constant presence. This framework acknowledges that what is desirable must also be grounded in what is possible within specific contexts, making feasibility a matter of balancing ethical imperatives and praxeological constraints with empirical realities. Institutional arrangements must be evaluated not only for their efficiency but also for their alignment with societal values and their capacity to adapt to unforeseen challenges. Such processes ensure that ideals, whether related to justice or functionality, are probed and adjusted in light of real-world outcomes, fostering both pragmatic and aspirational advances. What is desirable and what is feasible coevolve.

That being said, it is important to keep in mind that ultimately, not even the institutional epistemology framework situates institutional feasibility in the realm of blind institutional evolutions but at the intersection of institutional processes and epistemic and normative contributions from human agents. Institutions provide the structures and mechanisms for experimentation and adaptation, while agents use judgment and critical thinking to evaluate and refine these processes. In addressing the issue of feasibility, the role of human judgment and agency remains indispensable. While institutional frameworks and structures provide mechanisms for mobilizing knowledge and incentives, it is the human agent who drives the process of assessing and shaping these mechanisms. Through their judgment, individuals define criteria, interpret data, and oversee the ongoing adjustments necessary for institutions to remain responsive to real-world challenges, ensuring that institutions not only adapt but also align their evolution with broader social values and objectives. In brief, despite the emergence of the institutional epistemology approach, which endogenizes institutionally the ways of dealing with the feasibility issue, the role of the traditional human judgment-driven theoretical, philosophical, empirical, and methodological investigations and their associated conceptual and theoretical advances will continue to be the main driver of the process of responding to the challenges of the feasibility issue in bridging the gap between what is ideal and what is achievable.

References

Aligica, P. D. & Boettke, P. J. (2009). *Challenging Institutional Analysis and Development: The Bloomington School*. London Routledge.

Aligica, P. D. & Tarko, V. (2012). "Polycentricity: From Polanyi to Ostrom, and Beyond." *Governance*, 25(2), pp. 237–262.

Aligica, P. D. & Tarko, V. (2013). "Co-Production, Polycentricity and Value Heterogeneity: The Ostroms' Public Choice Institutionalism Revisited." *American Political Science Review*, 107(4), pp. 726-741.

Allen, M. (2006). "The Varieties of Capitalism Paradigm: Not Enough Variety?" *Socio-Economic Review*, 4(1), pp. 87–108.

Amable, B. (2003). *The Diversity of Modern Capitalism*. Oxford: Oxford University Press.

Amable, B. & Petit, P. (2001). "The Diversity of Social Systems of Innovation and Production during the 1990s." *Industrial and Corporate Change*, 10(4), pp. 173–197.

Anderson, E. (2010). *The Imperative of Integration*. Princeton, NJ: Princeton University Press.

Barry, N. P. (1988). *The Invisible Hand in Economics and Politics: A Study in the Two Conflicting Explanations of Society: End-States and Processes*. London: Institute of Economic Affairs.

Boettke, P. J. (2015a). *Why Perestroika Failed: The Politics and Economics of Socialist Transformation*. London: Routledge.

Boettke, P. J. (2015b). *Living Economics: Yesterday, Today, and Tomorrow*. Oakland, CA: Independent Institute.

Boettke, P. J. & Candela, R. A. (2015). "Rivalry, Polycentricism, and Institutional Evolution." In C. J. Coyne & V. H. Storr (eds.), *New Thinking in Austrian Political Economy*. Emerald Group, Advances in Austrian Economics, Vol. 19. Bingley: Emerald Group Publishing Limited, pp. 1–19.

Boettke, P. J. & Candela, R. A. (2023). "On the Feasibility of Technosocialism." *Journal of Economic Behavior & Organization*, 205, January, pp. 44–54.

Boettke, P. J. & Coyne, C. J. (2009). "Context Matters: Institutions and Entrepreneurship." *Foundations and Trends® in Entrepreneurship*, 5(3), pp. 135–209.

Boettke, P. & Fink, A. (2011). "Institutions First." *Journal of Institutional Economics*, 7(4), pp. 499–504.

Boettke, P. J., Coyne, C. J. & Leeson, P. T. (2014). "Hayek versus the Neoclassicists: Lessons from the Socialist Calculation Debate." In R. W. Garrison & N. P. Barry (eds.), *Elgar Companion to Hayekian Economics*. Cheltenham Edward Elgar, pp. 278–293.

Boettke, P. J., Lemke, J. S., & Palagashvili, L. (2015). "Polycentricity, Self-Governance, and the Art & Science of Association." *The Review of Austrian Economics*, 28, pp. 311–335.

Bromley, Daniel W. (2006). *Sufficient Reason: Volitional Pragmatism and the Meaning of Economic Institutions*. Princeton, NJ: Princeton University Press.

Buchanan, J. M. (2004). "Constitutional Political Economy." In *The Encyclopedia of Public Choice*. Boston, MA: Springer, pp. 60–67.

Bull, R. & Segerberg, K. (2001). "Basic Modal Logic." In Gabbay, D. M. & Guenthner, F. (eds.) *Handbook of Philosophical Logic, Vol. 3*. Amsterdam: Kluwer Academic, pp. 1–81.

Cernat, L. (2006). *Europeanization, Varieties of Capitalism and Economic Performance in Central and Eastern Europe*. Basingstoke: Palgrave Macmillan.

Clarke, K. A. & Primo, D. M. (2012). *A Model Discipline: Political Science and the Logic of Representations*. Oxford: Oxford University Press.

Coates, D. (2005). *Varieties of Capitalism, Varieties of Approaches*. Basingstoke: Palgrave Macmillan.

Coleman, J. S. (1990). *Foundations of Social Theory*. Cambridge, MA: Harvard University Press.

Crouch, C., Streeck, W., Boyer, R. et al. (2005). "Dialogue on 'Institutional Complementarity and Political Economy'." *Socio-Economic Review*, 3(2), pp. 359–382.

Estlund, D. (2014). *Utopophobia: Confronting the Limits (If Any) of Justice, Philosophy & Public Affairs*, 42(2), pp. 113–134.

Gaus, G. F. (2016). *The Tyranny of the Ideal: Justice in a Diverse Society*. Princeton, NJ: Princeton University Press.

Gheaus, A. (2013). "The Feasibility Constraint on the Concept of Justice." *The Philosophical Quarterly*, 63(252), pp. 445–464.

Gilabert, P. & Lawford-Smith, H. (2012). "Political Feasibility: A Conceptual Exploration." *Political Studies*, 60, pp. 809–825.

Gilbert, M. (2014). *Joint Commitment: How We Make the Social World*. Oxford: Oxford University Press.

Goodin, R. E. (1995). "Political Ideals and Political Practice." *British Journal of Political Science*, 44, pp. 635–646.

Goodin, R. E. & Tilly, C. (2008). *The Oxford Handbook of Contextual Political Analysis*. Oxford: Oxford University Press.

Hall, P. A. & Soskice, D. (2001). *Varieties of Capitalism: The Institutional Foundations of Comparative Advantage*. Oxford: Oxford University Press.

References

Hardin, R. (2002). *Trust and Trustworthiness*. New York, NY: Russell Sage Foundation.

Hayek, F. A. (1937). "Economics and Knowledge." *Economica*, 4(13), pp. 33–54.

Hayek, F. A. (2013 [1945]). "The Use of Knowledge in Society." In R. A. Epstein, G. L. Priest, & S. K. Komesar (eds.), *Modern Understandings of Liberty and Property*. London: Routledge, pp. 27–38.

Hayek, F. A. (1988). *The Fatal Conceit: The Errors of Socialism*. Ed. W. W. Bartley. London: Routledge.

Hayek, F. A. (2014). "The Facts of the Social Sciences." In B. J. Caldwell (ed.), *The Collected Works of F. A. Hayek, Vol 15: The Market and Other Orders*. Chicago, IL: The University of Chicago Press (pp. 57–70).

Hirschman, A. O. (1971). *A Bias for Hope: Essays on Development and Latin America*. New Haven, CT: Yale University Press.

Hodgson, G. M. (2015). "Much of the 'Economics of Property Rights' Devalues Property and Legal Rights." *Journal of Institutional Economics*, 11(4), pp. 683–709.

Hodgson, G. M. (2016). "Some Limitations of the Socialist Calculation Debate." *Journal of Contextual Economics–Schmollers Jahrbuch*, 136(1), pp. 33–57.

Koopmans, T. C. & Montias, J. M. (1971). "On the Description and Comparison of Economic Systems." In Eckstein, A. (ed.) *Comparison of Economic Systems: Theoretical and Methodological Approaches*. Berkeley: University of California Press, pp. 27–78.

Lange, O. (1936). "On the Economic Theory of Socialism. I." *The Review of Economic Studies*, 4(1), pp. 53–71.

Lange, O. (1937). "On the Economic Theory of Socialism. II." *The Review of Economic Studies*, 4(2), pp. 123–142.

Lane, D. & Myant, M. (2007). *Varieties of Capitalism in Post-Communist Countries*. Basingstoke: Palgrave Macmillan.

Lavoie, D. (1985). *Rivalry and Central Planning: The Socialist Calculation Debate Reconsidered (Vol. 22)*. Cambridge: Cambridge University Press.

Lawford-Smith, H. (2012). "Understanding Political Feasibility." *Journal of Political Philosophy*, 21(3), pp. 243–259.

Lipsey, R. G. & Lancaster, K. (1956). "The General Theory of Second Best." *The Review of Economic Studies*, 24(1), pp. 11–32.

Marwell, G. & Oliver, P. (1993). *The Critical Mass in Collective Action*. Cambridge: Cambridge University Press.

McMullin, E. (1985). "Galilean Idealization." *Studies in the History and Philosophy of Science*, 16, pp. 247–273.

Miller, G. J. (1992). *Managerial Dilemmas: The Political Economy of Hierarchy*. Cambridge: Cambridge University Press.

Müller, J. F. (2019). *Political Pluralism, Disagreement and Justice: The Case for Polycentric Democracy*. London: Routledge.

North, D. C. (1990). *Institutions, Institutional Change and Economic Performance*. Cambridge: Cambridge University Press.

North, D.C. (2005). *Understanding the Process of Economic Change*. Princeton, NJ: Princeton University Press.

Nove, A. (1991). *The Economics of Feasible Socialism Revisited*. London: Harper Collins Academic.

Oliver, P. E. & Marwell, G. (2001). "Whatever Happened to Critical Mass Theory? A Retrospective and Assessment." *Sociological Theory*, 19(3), pp. 292–311.

Ostrom, E. (1990). *Governing the Commons: The Evolution of Institutions for Collective Action*. Cambridge: Cambridge University Press.

Ostrom, E. (1998). "A Behavioral Approach to the Rational Choice Theory of Collective Action: Presidential Address, American Political Science Association, 1997." *American Political Science Review*, 92(1), pp. 1–22.

Ostrom, E. (1999). "Polycentricity, Complexity, and the Commons." *The Good Society*, 9(2), pp. 37–41.

Ostrom, E. (2000). "Collective Action and the Evolution of Social Norms." *Journal of Economic Perspectives*, 14(3), pp. 137–158.

Ostrom, E. (2005). *Understanding Institutional Diversity*. Princeton, NJ: Princeton University Press.

Ostrom, E. (2008). "Developing a Method for Analyzing Institutional Change." In Durlauf, S. N. & Blume, L. E. (eds.) *The New Palgrave Dictionary of Economics*. 2nd ed., Vol. 2. London: Palgrave Macmillan, pp. 595–599.

Ostrom, E. (2010). "Beyond Markets and States: Polycentric Governance of Complex Economic Systems." *American Economic Review*, 100, pp. 641–672.

Ostrom, V. (2014). "Polycentricity: The Structural Basis for Self-Governing Societies." In Sabetti, F. & Aligica, P. D. (eds.) *Choice, Rules and Collective Action: The Ostroms on the Study of Institutions and Governance*. Colchester: ECPR Press, pp. 103–124.

Ostrom, E., Gardner, R., & Walker, J. (1994). *Rules, Games, and Common-Pool Resources*. University of Ann Arbor: Michigan Press.

Pettit, P. & List, C. (2012). *Group Agents: The Possibility, Design, and Status of Corporate Agents*. Oxford: Oxford University Press.

Poteete, A. R., & Ostrom, E. (2004). "In Pursuit of Comparable Concepts and Data about Collective Action." *Agricultural Systems*, 82(3), pp. 215–232.

Pryor, F. L. (2005). "Comparative Economic Systems." In N. J. Smelser & P. B. Baltes (eds.), *International Encyclopedia of the Social & Behavioral Sciences* (Vol. 3). Amsterdam: Elsevier, pp. 2383–2391.

Rawls, J. (1971). *A Theory of Justice*. Cambridge, MA: The Belknap Press.

Rawls, J. (1999). *The Law of Peoples*. Cambridge, MA: Harvard University Press.

Rawls, J. (2001). *Justice as Fairness: A Restatement*. Cambridge, MA: Harvard University Press.

Rodrik, D. (2007). *One Economics, Many Recipes: Globalization, Institutions, and Economic Growth*. Princeton, NJ: Princeton University Press.

Room, G. (2011). *Complexity, Institutions and Public Policy: Agile Decision-Making in a Turbulent World*. Cheltenham: Edward Elgar.

Searle, J. R. (1995). *The Construction of Social Reality*. New York: Free Press.

Searle, J. R. (2010). *Making the Social World: The Structure of Human Civilization*. Oxford: Oxford University Press.

Southwood, N. (2018). "The Feasibility Issue." *Philosophy Compass*, 13(1), pp. 1–13.

Sugden, R. (2020). "The Community of Advantage." *Erasmus Journal for Philosophy and Economics*, 13(1), pp. 61–78.

Tuomela, R. (2013). *Social Ontology: Collective Intentionality and Group Agents*. Oxford: Oxford University Press.

Van Benthem, J. (2001). "Correspondence Theory." In Gabbay, D. M. & Guenthner, F. (eds.) *Handbook of Philosophical Logic, Vol. 3*. Amsterdam: Kluwer Academic, pp. 325–408.

Volacu, A. (2017). "Bridging Ideal and Non-Ideal Theory." *Political Studies*, 66(4), pp. 1–16.

Ward, B. (1967). *The Socialist Economy: A Study of Organizational Alternatives*. New York, NY: Random House.

Wiens, D. (2015a). "Against Ideal Guidance." *Journal of Politics*, 77(2), pp. 433–446.

Wiens, D. (2015b). "Political Ideals and the Feasibility Frontier." *Economics and Philosophy*, 31(3), pp. 447–477.

Williamson, O. E. (1985). *The Economic Institutions of Capitalism: Firms, Markets, Relational Contracting*. New York: Free Press.

Young, O. R. (2002). *The Drama of the Commons*. Washington, DC: National Academy Press.

References

Pope, H. C. (2005). "Competitive Economic Systems," in N. J. Smelser & P. B. Baltes (eds.), *International Encyclopedia of the Social & Behavioral Sciences* (vol. 4). Amsterdam: Elsevier, pp. 235-239.

Rawls, J. (1971). *A Theory of Justice*. Cambridge, MA: The Belknap Press.

Rawls, J. (1999). *The Law of Peoples*. Cambridge, MA: Harvard University Press.

Raz, J. (2001). *Engaging Reason: A Contemporary Approach*. MA: Harvard University Press.

Rodrik, D. (2007). *One Economics, Many Recipes: Globalization, Institutions, and Economic Growth*. Princeton, NJ: Princeton University Press.

Rodrik, D. (2011). *Globalization Paradox and Politics: Robbing Agile Democracy Must go together*. Lodeham Bhava-Uchikhnum Edward Elgar.

Searle, J. R. (1995). *The Construction of Social Reality*. New York: Free Press.

Searle, J. R. (2010). *Making the Social World: The Structure of Human Civilization*. Oxford: Oxford University Press.

Southwood, N. (2018). "The Feasibility Issue," *Philosophy Compass*, 13(7), pp. 1-13.

Stephen, R. (2020). "The Community the Assemblage: A Social Journal for Philosophy and Economics," 13(1), pp. 61-76.

Tuomela, R. (2013). *Social Ontology: Collective Intentionality and Group Agents*. Oxford: Oxford University Press.

Van Parijs, P. et al. (2017). *What's Wrong with a Free Lunch?* Boston: Beacon Press.

Cambridge Elements⁼

Austrian Economics

Peter Boettke
George Mason University

Peter Boettke is a Professor of Economics & Philosophy at George Mason University, the BB&T Professor for the Study of Capitalism, and the director of the F. A. Hayek Program for Advanced Study in Philosophy, Politics and Economics at the Mercatus Center at George Mason University.

About the Series

This series will primarily be focused on contemporary developments in the Austrian School of Economics and its relevance to the methodological and analytical debates at the frontier of social science and humanities research, and the continuing relevance of the Austrian School of Economics for the practical affairs of public policy throughout the world.

Austrian Economics

Elements in the Series

The Decline and Rise of Institutions: A Modern Survey of the Austrian Contribution to the Economic Analysis of Institutions
Liya Palagashvili, Ennio Piano and David Skarbek

Austrian Capital Theory: A Modern Survey of the Essentials
Peter Lewin and Nicolas Cachanosky

Public Debt as a Form of Public Finance: Overcoming a Category Mistake and Its Vices
Richard E. Wagner

Defense, Peace, and War Economics
Christopher J. Coyne

Cultural Considerations within Austrian Economics
Virgil Storr and Arielle John

The Origins and Consequences of Property Rights: Austrian, Public Choice, and Institutional Economics Perspectives
Meina Cai, Llia Murtazashvili, Colin Harris and Jennifer Murtazashvili

The Political Economy of Public Pensions
Eileen Norcross and Daniel J. Smith

The Political Economy of Terrorism, Counterterrorism, and the War on Terror
Anne R. Bradley, Christopher J. Coyne and Abigail R. Hall

Understanding Ludwig Lachmann's Economics
Virgil Henry Storr and Solomon M. Stein

James Buchanan and Peaceful Cooperation: From Public Finance to a Theory of Collective Action
Alain Marciano

The Socialist Calculation Debate: Theory, History, and Contemporary Relevance
Peter Boettke, Rosolino A. Candela and Tegan L. Truitt

Institutional Diversity and the Economic Calculation Debate: The Feasibility Issue Revisited
Paul Dragos Aligica and Adrian Miroiu

A full series listing is available at: www.cambridge.org/EAEC

Printed by Libri Plureos GmbH in Hamburg, Germany